OSCAR and LUCINDA
THE SCREENPLAY

Laura Jones wrote the original screenplay for *High Tide*, directed by Gillian Armstrong. Her other credits include *An Angel At My Table* and *The Portrait Of A Lady*, both directed by Jane Campion and *The Well*, directed by Samantha Lang. She lives in Sydney.

OSCAR *and* LUCINDA

THE SCREENPLAY

LAURA JONES

BASED ON THE NOVEL BY PETER CAREY

University of Queensland Press

First published 1998 by University of Queensland Press
Box 42, St Lucia, Queensland 4067 Australia

Text and photographs TM and © 1998
Twentieth Century Fox Film Corporation,
Australian Film Finance Corporation Limited,
New South Wales Film and Television Office,
and Dalton Films Pty, Limited

Photographs by Stephen Morley (UK) and
Philip Le Mesurier (Australian)

Laura Jones is hereby identified as author of this work

Printed in Australia by McPherson's Printing Group

Cataloguing in Publication Data
National Library of Australia

Jones, Laura, 1951– .
Oscar & Lucinda : the screenplay.

1. Carey, Peter, 1943– . Oscar and Lucinda. I. Title. II.
Title: Oscar & Lucinda (Motion picture).

791.4372

ISBN 0 7022 3045 6

CONTENTS

Oscar and Lucinda

EXT. BOAT HARBOUR. NEW SOUTH WALES (NSW). THE PRESENT
DAY

*A little weatherboard church with corrugated iron roof journeys – by
unseen means – away from us. Its paint a faded chalky lime-green.
The sky behind it a deep blue.*

> NARRATOR
> (*voice-over*)
> I would have no story to tell you,

*The church now revealed to be on a large low-loader grinding up a
grassy rise.*

*The Narrator – bright red hair, only seen from behind – walks between
old timber foundation stumps of church.*

*His feet crunch on broken glass amongst the weeds. He bends and
picks up a piece of glass.*

> if my great-grandfather had not wagered everything to bring
> that church here.

EXT. MITCHELL'S CREEK. NSW. 1848. DAY

> NARRATOR
> (*voice-over*)
> Or if Lucinda had not been given a Prince Rupert's drop.

*A little wooden box held by a child. The child's hand lifts the lid to
reveal: a glass drop, with its bulbous rounded head narrowing to a thin
sinuous tail, lying in a bed of sawdust.*

*Lucinda – seven and neat as a pin except for unruly reddish-brown
hair – looking down at the drop:*

> ABEL/ELIZABETH
> Happy Birthday!

Elizabeth, Lucinda's mother, and Abel, her father, both have smooth straight black hair. Elizabeth holds an axe and Abel a hammer.

Lucinda is taking the drop out of its box:

Careful! Not too tight! Gently!

Lucinda holds up the drop by its nose:

ELIZABETH

Here.

Lucinda carefully places the drop where her mother indicates: in the middle of the chopping block.

Abel lifts his hammer and brings it down, bang! on to the delicate glass drop.

The drop is still, miraculously, perfect.

ABEL

You see? Even with a hammer!

ELIZABETH

I'll try the axe.

Elizabeth swings her axe down on to the fragile drop. It bounces and lands: still its perfect self.

Elizabeth and Abel turn to Lucinda:

ABEL

Lucinda?

Lucinda takes out pliers from her apron pocket. Holds drop by point, staring at its delicate beauty close up.

Lucinda slowly puts drop into plier's jaws. Her face pulled tight.

Her parents wait.

LUCINDA

I like it just as it is.

ELIZABETH/ABEL

Go on. Take the plunge. You'll see.

Lucinda – with both hands – squeezes the pliers tightly shut.

As the glass explodes in a crescendo of light.

EXT. HEADLAND. DEVON. 1848. DAY

Oscar – seven and thin with flame-red hair – in flannelette nightgown, runs bare-footed down steep overgrown red mud path leading from wild headland to beach:

NARRATOR
(*voice-over*)

My great-grandfather had skin like his mother's.

He slithers on mud and grabs hold of gorsey undergrowth to stop his fall, then runs on:

EXT. BEACH. DEVON. 1848. DAY

NARRATOR
(*voice-over*)

Although the cancer had been removed by acid dropped on to her tender skin, she had died anyway.

Theophilus Hopkins – dark and sinewy with black hair and full beard

– runs full-pelt down the beach. He carries a swag of his dead wife's clothes, still on their wooden hangers. He is weeping.

He runs straight into the sea, working against the incoming tide. A few clothes drop as he goes. Chest-high in the water, he throws the clothes away, out to sea.

The sea won't take them. The current washes the clothes back against the man. He tries to push them away from himself, weeping, calling out for them to go, go, take them.

A new sound makes him turn: he sees, on the shore, the figure of his son. His voice faint across the water:

OSCAR
(*calls*)

Papa!

Oscar on shore. His feet on stones of beach. The mounds of black shining seaweed sinister to him.

Papa!

His father wading back towards him, his urgent movements hampered by the sea.

His wife's clothes a jumbled mass, coming in on the tide, and Theophilus has to part them to get back to his son.

Oscar looks down, with fear, at one of his mother's blouses about to wrap around his ankles: its arms floating out on the water, moving, as if alive.

Oscar runs backwards, away from the blouse. The sea, from now on, will always smell of death to him. The sound of Theophilus preaching:

THEOPHILUS
(*voice-over*)
It shall be a day like any other of the Almighty's days.

EXT. BRETHREN MEETING HOUSE. DEVON. 1856. DAY

As we look up at the uncompromisingly plain facade – built from Devon limestone – of the Brethren Meeting Rooms:

THEOPHILUS
(*voice-over*)
We are free to go about our ordinary business, in our houses,

INT. BRETHREN MEETING ROOMS. DEVON. 1856. DAY

Oscar – now fourteen – concentrates on his father as he preaches, in a loud ringing voice to the small congregation of Plymouth Brethren: mainly farm workers, thatchers, warreners, and fishermen.

THEOPHILUS
(*voice-over*)
in the fields and lanes round about. There will be no mockery of the Almighty with pagan rituals. Others may judge and laugh but they are in a darkness of their own making and will burn in hell. 'And the light shineth in darkness, and the darkness comprehended it not.' Nay, we shall not use the name that others confer upon it, the Popish name, Christ's Mass.

INT. HOPKINS'S COTTAGE. DEVON. 1856. DAY

Cottage on headland. Sky all greys, windblown trees, red mud tracks. Sound of the sea below. Faint sound of Christmas Day church bells ringing.

> NARRATOR
> (*voice-over*)
> If it were not for a Christmas pudding, I would not have been born.

INT. HOPKINS'S COTTAGE. DEVON. 1856. DAY

Bells continue and finish, during:

A wooden tray, divided into small compartments, sits on a broad window ledge. It is filled with buttons: their colours enticing against the grey day through the cold glass of the uncurtained dining-room window.

At the dining table Oscar and Theophilus eat their companionable but plain lunch: stew, cabbage, potatoes and water.

> THEOPHILUS
> You have re-classified your mama's buttons.

> OSCAR
> Yes, father.

> THEOPHILUS
> The taxonomic principle being colour, with the spectrum from left to right.

> OSCAR
> With size the second principle of order.

> THEOPHILUS
> Very good.

Mrs Williams coming out of kitchen, vigorously brushing her wild grey hair as she goes to the dining-room door.

Out of sight of the dining-room she continues to brush her hair as she waits for Theophilus and Oscar to finish grace: 'Amen'. Brush into apron pocket, she steps into doorway:

MRS WILLIAMS

Excuse me, sir. Would Master Hopkins help me with the pollard for the pig's swill?

Oscar looks at his father, who nods permission.

Oscar follows an excited, even secretive, Mrs Williams back to the kitchen.

INT. KITCHEN. HOPKINS'S COTTAGE. 1856. DAY

Fanny Drabble, the kitchen-hand, holds a white plate. On it is a steaming Christmas pudding, the size of an orange, cut into quarters.

Oscar stares at it, his nostrils soaking up the fragrant smell.

Mrs Williams takes the plate from Fanny and holds it out to Oscar.

MRS WILLIAMS

Here.

OSCAR

What is it?

FANNY

Christmas pudding.

MRS WILLIAMS

For you. Eat up.

Oscar lifts a spoonful to his mouth. He treasures the exotic deliciousness of it.

Mrs Williams and Fanny Drabble – smiling, smiling – can't take their eyes off him.

Oscar – almost sleepy with pleasure – has just taken a second spoonful when:

Theophilus strides into kitchen.

He hits the back of Oscar's head. Spoon drops to floor. Theophilus grasps the back of Oscar's head, thumb and fingers pressed into neck, a hand under Oscar's mouth. Oscar tries to swallow. Theophilus again thumps the back of his head. Oscar spits out the pudding, into Theophilus's hand.

Theophilus picks up pudding on plate.

Holds it out with revulsion to the women and the boy:

THEOPHILUS

This is the food of Satan.

And throws the pudding, from the plate, into the fire.

Oscar has tasted the pudding and does not believe his father.

Theophilus turns from the fire.

FANNY

But, sir, it be Christmas Day.

THEOPHILUS

Some call it that, but none in my employ.

Oscar sees the injustice of this in Fanny's cowed look.

Well, Master Hopkins, you will be a good helper and fetch up the specimen buckets.

Now, anger subsiding, Theophilus sees the blue marks on his son's neck. He sees his son's eyes, and knows the damage he has done.

EXT. PATH/BEACH. DEVON. 1856. DAY

On the mid-winter beach – all greys, except for the soft reds of the limestone cliffs – we look up to the little track winding its way down the rough wind-blown headland. Two distant figures descend:

Theophilus, bulky in brown oilskin, is almost at the beach.

Near the top of the track we see Oscar's red hair as he hurries down after his father.

On the track with Oscar, looking down to:

Theophilus crossing the stony beach, the sea grey and pearly, the black mounds of washed-up seaweed.

Oscar, encumbered with six roped buckets, three hessian bags, coils of rope, ritualistically counts his steps down to the beach:

. . . two hundred and forty, forty-one, forty-two —

He stumbles and slides on the red mud track, buckets clanging. He stands and counts on, making up for the slide:

. . . forty-eight, forty-nine . . .

Theophilus, chest-high in water of rock-pool, chips specimens from cliff-face. Strands of seaweed ripple out in the water around him. He glances for a second across to his son, a small figure huddled against the cliff.

Oscar sits, swaddled in four sweaters, skin blue with cold, knees drawn up, back against the limestone cliff, as far away as possible from where the sea breaks over the rock ledge. His filled specimen buckets beside him: sea-creatures gliding in water.

Oscar's continuing anger: hand up to red, burning ear, his bruised neck. He prays:

Dear God, if it is your desire that your flock eat pudding in celebration of Thy birth as a man, then show Thy humble supplicant a sign.

Oscar opens his eyes: nothing.

The sky remains unchanged. Silence except for the sound of wind across water, the suck and hiss of the tide.

Dear God, if it be Thy will that Thy people eat pudding, smite him!

Again, no sign.

But Theophilus is now wading back towards the pool's edge. Oscar stands to help his father.

At the pool's edge, Theophilus hauls himself out of the water, groaning with the weight of the heavy buckets lashed around his oilskin.

Oscar bends to untie ropes holding buckets, and sees:

Theophilus smitten: bleeding. His thigh gashed. Thick red blood rises through blue serge of trouser leg. In the water is the red stain of Theophilus's blood.

(*voice-over*)

Oscar was frightened by what he had begun.

EXT. HIGH PATH. DEVON. 1856. DAY

Oscar crouches on high path outside town. Northern wind blows.

He is drawing with a yellow stone on to a rocky part of the little path.

He whispers to himself as he draws in the symbols:

OSCAR

Father . . . Baptists . . . Catholics . . . Anglicans.

Oscar adds a head and tail, and quickly fills in the two bottom squares with a nought, and an omega for end, to disguise the meaning.

NARRATOR
(*voice-over*)

Now his father no longer knew the true will of God, Oscar devised a way of asking the question directly.

Oscar stands, facing away from the yellow markings, his heels against the Omega square:

OSCAR

Show me a sign that Thou talkest to me.

He throws the yellow tor over his left shoulder.

It lands on Alpha.

Oscar turns and stares at the tor's message, his heart heavy.

Please, dear God, no.

EXT. VARIOUS PATHS/ROCKS. DEVON. 1856. DAY

Oscar's tor spins through the air and lands on the Alpha square of the yellow markings, freshly drawn in another spot, on another day.

Oscar's dismay.

The tor lands again – another time, another place – on Alpha. And again. And again

NARRATOR
(*voice-over*)

God repeated the message again and again: Alpha equals
Anglican.

*Oscar picks up the tor and puts it in his pocket. He scumbles the yellow
markings with his boot, only partly erasing them, then turns and fights
against the wind, down the rocky path.*

EXT. PATH/ANGLICAN VICARAGE. DEVON. 1856. DAY

Oscar runs along path, ritualistically counting steps out aloud.

*He stops at a place on the path high above the Anglican vicarage next
door to its square church tower. He looks down into the vicarage
garden, where he watches the figures of a man and a woman.*

NARRATOR
(*voice-over*)

This was where God wished him to go.

EXT. ANGLICAN VICARAGE. DEVON. 1856. DAY

*Hugh Stratton – a tall, stooped forty, with floppy fringe of fair straight
hair and a boyish face – pokes a long stick into cracks in masonry
of vicarage. His wife, Betty – a large-boned, flaxen-haired woman
with a forward-tilting walk – beside him.*

HUGH

But it is new, Betty, a new crack. Look.

BETTY

Stop, you will only make it worse.

HUGH

They appear overnight. Did you see what was in the plate
today?

BETTY

The walls have always been damp, Hugh, and we have not
died from it.

HUGH

That Dissenter steals our congregation one by one. We will
have no one left, while he grows fat.

A noise makes them turn:

*Outrageously, Oscar stands, balancing arms-out, on their high stone
wall. He stares down at them, across the meagre vegetable beds.*

That's his boy!

BETTY

Hugh, your back.

*Hugh starts to run towards Oscar, fuelled with anger against
Theophilus, who has stolen his congregation and caused the rot in
his house.*

*He clears the vegetable beds, one by one, as if hurdling. He has not
run like this since Eton.*

*Oscar drops from the wall to the ground. He steps across a vegetable
bed towards hurdling Hugh.*

They face each other, panting Hugh stopped by tomato stakes.

HUGH

You, boy, go home.

Oscar takes a step back, on to a lettuce.

Off my lettuces.

Oscar takes another step back, on to another lettuce.

OSCAR

Wait!

HUGH

Off!

OSCAR

I am called.

*The man and boy stare at each other, both impressed by the conviction
in Oscar's voice.*

INT. ANGLICAN VICARAGE. DEVON. 1856. DAY

A row of raisins, spaced precisely apart, lines the rim of a willow-pattern plate. Oscar removes another raisin from the alien food on his plate and places it with the other rejects.

He sits, wrongly it seems to him, at the head of the dining-room table, in the shadowy, shabby vicarage dining-room. Evening light and the lamps not yet on. Hugh and Betty Stratton sit on either side of him. Hugh drinks sherry.

> BETTY
>
> They are only raisins.

> HUGH
>
> He is probably unfamiliar with them.

> BETTY
>
> What will your poor father do? Think of the pain you will cause him.

> OSCAR
>
> I know, but he is in error, you see. He is not saved.

Betty looks at Hugh: instead of anxiety she sees a beneficent smile.

But still, you will go home to him. Hugh?

OSCAR
I cannot. No matter how I want to.

BETTY
But surely your father loves you?

OSCAR
Yes, very much. I also love him.

Betty has not seen this calm and powerful look on Hugh's face for years.

BETTY
But, Hugh, the cost.

HUGH
The boy is called.

BETTY
In what sense, 'called'?

HUGH
He is called to Holy Orders.

BETTY
You have had three glasses, Hugh.

HUGH
I shall coach him in his Articles, Betty. He will go to my old College. Think of that.

Betty, against her will, charmed by Hugh's boyish smile: so rare now.

Oscar sees, from the window:

A little group of Plymouth Brethren, kneeling in the long grass outside the vicarage, praying for his return.

EXT. DAM. MITCHELL'S CREEK. NSW. 1859. DAY

Under a big hot sky: paddocks and wheatfields, carved out of bush, stretch out around a little dam:

(voice-over)

Elizabeth knew that she had produced a proud square peg in the full knowledge that from coast to coast there were nothing but round holes.

Lucinda – now almost seventeen – breaststrokes in the dam. Her undershirt balloons up around her. Her cropped hair wet. She is reciting in French, in rhythm to her swimming. She turns on her back, propelling herself through the water.

INT. FARMHOUSE. MITCHELL'S CREEK. NSW. 1859. DAY

Elizabeth writes in her journal at the table in the cottage's main room.

A little collection, amongst the crowded shelves of books, of glass jars and bottles and curiosities: amber, blue, green, clear, red and violet.

Lucinda comes into the cottage, carrying unwashed eggs in a tin bowl.

LUCINDA

Eight eggs. I went for a swim.

Elizabeth continues writing, as:

ELIZABETH

We should have returned home after your father's death.

Lucinda is puzzled:

LUCINDA

Returned home?

ELIZABETH

To England.

Elizabeth reaches for a shawl and, in spite of the hot day, wraps it around her shoulders.

I can tolerate what I've done to myself, by staying on, but I cannot bear to think what I have done to you.

LUCINDA

Mama!

Lucinda, puzzled by her mother's tone, laughs and bends down to hug her. She feels her mother's hot skin:

You are so hot.

ELIZABETH

I am freezing.

EXT. QUADRANGLE. NEW COLLEGE OXFORD. 1865. DAY

From out of the darkness of a passageway comes the sound of running feet, heavy breathing.

Five young men, carrying hockey sticks – one also with a sack – run out in a tight, intent little posse, excited by their purpose.

They cut across a courtyard and disappear through a door.

INT. OSCAR'S ROOM. NEW COLLEGE OXFORD. 1865. DAY

A bleak room with only one straight chair, table and bed. Oscar's mother's buttons in tray, tilted on mantel over fireplace with empty grate.

Oscar – now twenty-four – crouches at felt-covered board where he pins hand-written sheets of complicated study-notes. He is humming a hymn: high and tuneful.

We hear, although Oscar appears not to, the sound of running feet coming upstairs, muffled laughter and thuds.

A loud BANG! BANG! on the door startles Oscar.

As he crosses to open the door, the sound comes again.

Innocent of trouble, Oscar opens the door wide, to:

The group of men, with hockey sticks and sack, burst in, forcing Oscar aside as they take over his room: everything happens at once.

MAN 1

Yay, Odd Bod! Hunt's on!

MAN 2

Here's sport for you! Grab a stick!

Put him in goal! Corner him! Odd Bod, Bod, Bod!

Another man makes hunting cries, joined by others.

The door banged shut behind them. Oscar confused.

And, in the chaos: the tray holding Oscar's mother's buttons is knocked over, buttons spill everywhere, the sack is tipped up and the rats begin to emerge, and a great war-cry from the young men as they raise their hockey sticks.

EXT. FARM. MITCHELL'S CREEK. NSW. 1859. DAY

Surveyors checking sight-lines through the orchard. Red surveyor's pegs already thread through the long grass, felled trees around them.

The sound of men calling, of axes and mattocks, as trees are chopped, stumps grubbed from the earth.

Lucinda, wearing a bloomer costume in funeral black, and carrying a little case, hears the sound – unfamiliar out here – of axes and men's voices as she climbs a rise, paddocks stretching out behind her.

She hurries to the top and looks down to the orchard and sees, with a shock, the start of its destruction.

EXT. FARM. MITCHELL'S CREEK. NSW. 1859. DAY

On the verandah, Lucinda is confronting Mr Ahearn, Elizabeth's solicitor – a big man of sixty-two, but soft and awkward – who has surveyor's plans unrolled in his large hands. Lucinda holds a legal document.

Ahearn's wife hovers, and their horse and trap waits in the yard beyond. The sound of axes and men at work carries faintly up to them.

> LUCINDA
> She would have talked of it to me.

> AHEARN
> She intended to return Home.

Lucinda confused.

> LUCINDA
> This is our home.

> AHEARN
> To England.

> LUCINDA
> This is not my mother's signature.

> AHEARN
> Indeed it is. She signed it in my office.

Ahearn once again tries to hold the plans out in front of her, but she will not look.

> She had it all calculated. Five farms, you see, of four
> thousand acres apiece –

> LUCINDA
> (*over*)
> You say everything is mine?

> AHEARN
> Held in trust by me.

> LUCINDA
> My mother would not have done that.

AHEARN

Dear little girl. With a fortune such as this you will be married in a jiffy.

Mrs Ahearn, at little signals from her husband, has now joined Mr Ahearn and this odd girl.

LUCINDA

Why was I not told this?

AHEARN

I would have told you, after your mother's funeral, all in good time.

MRS AHEARN

If you had not run away.

LUCINDA

I am staying here.

AHEARN

You cannot. Your new home is with Mrs Ahearn and myself, in Parramatta.

His wife puts a tentative arm around Lucinda as:

MRS AHEARN

You will go to Mrs Cousin's School for Young Ladies.

And now Mrs Ahearn and Mr Ahearn, one on either side of Lucinda, are trying to lead her down the verandah steps towards their trap.

LUCINDA

Do not touch me.

Lucinda violently reaches out and grabs hold of the verandah post.

AHEARN

Come come, girlie.

MRS AHEARN

Oh, dear.

They try to ease her away, but she grasps the post more tightly, she will not budge. The force of her will frightens the Ahearns, unused to displays of powerful emotions.

AHEARN

You will be rich one day.

LUCINDA

I do not want to be rich. That is not the point.

She finally cries, hands around the verandah post, leaning against it.

Mr Ahearn creeps to her suitcase, in the open doorway, and picks it up and stands waiting: it will only be a matter of time.

INT. STAIRCASE. NEW COLLEGE OXFORD. 1865. DAY

Wardley-Fish – a good-looking, robust young man with a fair beard trimmed to show the line of his jaw – runs, hands in pockets, stick under arm, humming, up an inner staircase.

He knocks with stick on door: Bang! Bang!

INT. OSCAR'S ROOM. NEW COLLEGE OXFORD. 1865. DAY

Oscar, having learned his lesson, crosses cautiously to the sound of banging on his door.

He peers out of the half-open door. Both Fish and Oscar equally surprised to see the other.

FISH

I say, these are West's rooms.

OSCAR

West? No, Fish, they are –

FISH
(*over*)

He has new rooms on this staircase. Dammit. I'm sure the Scout said . . . two . . . it . . . or maybe it was one . . .

Oscar holds his door open wide.

OSCAR

Come in.

Fish steps in, looks around: made uneasy by the room's sparse gloominess. He is shocked by it, oddly embarrassed.

FISH

I say, Odd Bod, do you like a flutter?

He immediately regrets it.

OSCAR

A flutter, Fish?

FISH
(*answers himself*)

Of course you don't.

Oscar – determined to make a friend of someone who has come without malice, although by mistake – pushes a chair towards Fish, who ignores it, as:

OSCAR

What is this 'flutter'?

FISH

It is to do with the racetrack.

OSCAR

Athletics?

Oscar sits on bed, to encourage Fish to sit in chair.

FISH

Horse-races.

OSCAR

Horses! And which part of the race involves the flutter?

FISH
(*barks*)

A wager, a bet, a flutter.
(*gentler*)

You do know what a bet is?

OSCAR

No, Fish, I don't.

Fish wants to escape. He will miss his day at the track.

FISH

You give money to chaps and if the horse you like is the one that wins, then they give you double your money back, or treble, or whatever.

OSCAR
(*astonished*)

Treble your money for guessing?

FISH

Guessing correctly. You mock me.

OSCAR

No, Fish. It is new to me. I was raised in a little village in Devon, very much out of the way.

FISH

Look here, Odd Bod, I have to dash.

OSCAR

Perhaps you could call me Hopkins.

FISH

Call you what?

Fish barely stops at the door.

OSCAR

My name. Hopkins.

Fish looks directly at Oscar for a second: he is surprised to be oddly moved by Oscar's fine trusting face.

EXT. THE PADDOCK. EPSOM DOWNS. 1865. DAY

The coloured silks of the jockeys, high up on their horses, being led by stablehands and trainers around the paddock. The beautiful rippling coats of the horses, their high-bred temperaments intoxicating to Oscar – jingling the coins in his pocket – standing with excitable Fish in front of crowd in paddock:

FISH

Do not rattle your sovereigns. You are not a plunger.

26

OSCAR

What is a — ?

FISH

A plunger? West is a plunger. He starts with a couple of sovs, comes up trumps, then dabs it all down on the second and loses the lot.

Fish drags Oscar forward:

Look at her. Look! Revenger's Lass, three to one in the fourth. It's the day for a powerful bum like that.

The horse, startled, dances sideways, turns, backs towards Oscar and Fish, who are forced back into the crowd, as:

Look at that backside. Just look!

Oscar has nowhere else to look.

Oscar, following Fish, runs through the crowd. He has never seen such an astonishing variety of people.

Fish stops to take out his brandy flask.

He looks at Oscar and recognizes his intoxicated smile.

You have caught the germ.

Takes swig. Offers flask to Oscar's headshake 'no'.

I am corrupting you.

OSCAR

No, Fish, don't you see?

FISH

You should not be here.

OSCAR

You are an agent of the Lord.

FISH

Whoa, Odd Bod, ease up.

OSCAR

I have been praying to God for funds. Now I shall be able to pay my bills.

Fish looks with misgiving at Oscar's intense, pure face, his red hair wilder than usual.

FISH

Quick, or we'll miss the first. I am already damned, of course.

EXT. BOOKMAKERS' ENCLOSURE. EPSOM DOWNS. 1865. DAY

Bookmakers call their prices as race-goers crowd around each bookie, placing their bets. The odds chalked and re-chalked on to the boards, money and betting tickets passing hands.

Oscar watches as Fish pushes his over-heated way into crowd around a bookie. Turns for a second to urgently wave Oscar in with him.

Oscar shakes his head 'no'. Shuts his eyes for a brief second in silent prayer. Then makes his way to a different bookie.

As he slides into the crowd, only his red hair visible to us as he works his way further in, joining the punters around his chosen bookie:

NARRATOR
(*voice-over*)

My great-grandfather won his first bet. In the case-histories

of pathological gamblers, you find the same story told time
and time again.

EXT. QUADRANGLE. NEW COLLEGE OXFORD. 1865. DAY

*Hugh, although his sciatica hurts this morning, walks swiftly out of a
door into New College quadrangle. Red mud on his shoes and trouser
cuffs.*

He passes Wardley-Fish on the path.

INT. OSCAR'S ROOM. NEW COLLEGE OXFORD. 1865. DAY

*Oscar holds out his hand for Hugh's coat, but Hugh is already draping
it across the bed, as:*

HUGH

You have paid your buttery bill. I enquired.

He lifts lid off tea-pot: part of Oscar's spartan breakfast.

And drinking coffee.

OSCAR

No, not coffee.

HUGH

Not? I bring you a question. It is this. Do you have an
income? No, thank you, I would rather stand. I would take it
very ill if you had tricked me.

OSCAR

I have not tricked you.

HUGH

It is fifteen years since I could afford coffee, and now you,
a poor creature who has nothing in the world but what I can
scrape together, are so gracious as to send me this luxury.

OSCAR

I only wish you not to worry. God will provide for me. Did
you enjoy your –?

HUGH

Do not, I beg you, be so simple. You are poisoned with your father's ideas.

OSCAR

I may be simple –

HUGH

Your father is paying.

OSCAR

I swear he is not. He would not pay a penny to send me here. We have met only three times since we parted.

HUGH

Then where does the money come from?

Oscar, about to tell the truth, stops as he thinks of his father hearing of it.

I am raising money here, in Oxford, for my little church's restoration. You must promise me you would never be involved in anything amiss. I cannot have my name brought low.

Oscar lightly touches Hugh's rigid shoulder.

OSCAR

My dear patron, there is no need for such a promise.

Hugh stares hard at Oscar, it almost seems with hatred.

HUGH

For years we scrape and save to support you and now I am losing my health worrying about how to support you here.

OSCAR

No need at all.

Hugh's face suddenly softens, he relaxes.

HUGH

I know you are a good boy, Oscar. I do know that.

Oscar and Fish – wearing their racetrack clothes – in porch of church. Oscar dividing a large wad of notes into big and small portions. As he goes to put the small portion into his pocket, Fish grabs his hand.

FISH

Stop. More for you, less for the poor.

OSCAR

This is all I need.

FISH

You need new togs.

OSCAR

What is wrong with my togs?

FISH

Everything.

Oscar laughs and puts big wad of notes into poor box. Fish groans.

You rake it in then throw it away. Look at you. You look like a scarecrow.

Oscar, more puzzled than hurt, looks down at his clothes.

OSCAR

Perhaps because I am wearing your coat.

Fish groans, turns his face to the wall and leans against it, almost weeping with laughter. Oscar puzzled, but pleased to have amused his friend. A dog stands barking at Fish.

INT. OSCAR'S ROOM. NEW COLLEGE OXFORD. 1865. NIGHT

Night in Oscar's room, as spartan as ever. Rows of white envelopes stacked in shoebox on his table. Piles of blue betting slips on which Oscar writes racetrack details. He puts a pile of betting slips into an envelope and adds it to the shoebox. He opens a black clothbound notebook, halfway through, to a partly-filled page of minutely written racetrack information. Adds that day's entry. All the time he hums a hymn.

EXT. STEAMER/WHARVES. SYDNEY HARBOUR. NSW. 1865. DAY

A little steamer makes its way into Sydney Harbour.

NARRATOR
(*voice-over*)

Lucinda had never been on a boat. She had never been to Sydney. She carried with her a bank draft for her entire fortune, as well as an itchy impatience to grasp what her mother had called the working world.

Lucinda – surrounded by stacked boxes of pale cauliflowers – sits on a packing case in bow of steamer. She looks out at Sydney, nervously excited by the adventure of her unknown future. She wears a cape over her irritating new crinoline, a new hat covers her scraped-up hair. She holds a little beaded purse.

As the steamer is swung about, Lucinda sees a sign: PRINCE RUPERT'S GLASSWORKS.

Lucinda's face as she remembers the Prince Rupert's drop she exploded with her parents.

Lucinda knew that glass is a thing in disguise,

A FOR SALE *sign on the glassworks. The works are in shadow. They look intimidating, almost evil, to Lucinda, as she passes by on the steamer. Lucinda takes out little notebook from purse and writes down the name:*

is not solid at all, but a liquid, and even while it is as frail as the ice on a Parramatta puddle, it is stronger than Sydney sandstone. She did not need to be told that it is as good a material as any to build a life on.

EXT. STEAMER/WHARVES. SYDNEY HARBOUR. NSW. 1865. DAY

At the noisy crowded wharf, the steamer Captain shakes Lucinda's hand:

CAPTAIN

Good luck, miss.

Self-conscious, awkward, she hands him two sixpences.

One is more than enough, miss.

Lucinda apologizes and unhappily takes back one of the sixpences. The Captain hands her a cauliflower with a little bow. She takes its heavy cool weight in one hand.

Lucinda, awkward in wretched crinoline, with heavy suitcase in one hand, cauliflower in the other, walks through crowd on wharf: she is the only woman and feels she is being stared at. Self-conscious, her crinoline violently off-centre, her suitcase banging her leg, she disappears into the crowd on the wharf.

EXT. VICARAGE. SYDNEY. 1865. DAY

The vicarage of All Saints in Woollahra is one of the most coveted in the colony.

INT. VICARAGE. SYDNEY. 1865. DAY

The Reverend Dennis Hasset – a tall well-made man with dark hair, often called handsome – examines a letter from Lucinda, talking to his servant Frazer, a spare sandy Yorkshireman.

> HASSET
> If this Frenchman . . . Leplastrier . . . if he expects to find an expert on glass I am afraid he will find only an enthusiast.

He looks, with some vanity, around his study: three lamps burning, a fire in the grate.

> However! He has found out my little hobby and I shall try to advise.

As Hasset artfully re-arranges a piece of glass cullet, like a large chunk of diamond, in a spot on his desk where it catches the light:

> I wonder if I shall have to use my rather rusty French.

> FRAZER
> If the gentleman has no English, sir, I would be pleased to translate.

> HASSET
> I didn't know you spoke the lingo, Frazer. There is the door.

As Frazer leaves the room:

FRAZER

Oui, monsieur, certainement,

Hasset amused, a little miffed, as Frazer leaves. He listens to the faint sounds of Frazer and his visitor, as he readjusts the lamp on his desk.

Frazer appears in the doorway:

Your visitor, sir.

HASSET

Jolly good, show him in.

He is surprised, but not shocked, to see Lucinda. Although her grey silk bloomer costume and her unexpected youth unsettles him, he is delighted by her.

Ah, *Monsieur* Leplastrier.

Lucinda awkward, blushing, does not understand his joke. Has she made a mistake? But her embarrassment disappears as her eye is caught by the light from the glass cullet.

INT. VICARAGE. SYDNEY. 1865. DAY

Lucinda holds up a piece of blue glass to the light.

Hasset's unease is almost forgotten in their shared passion for glass. He hands her two lenses:

HASSET

This is from Botany and the other from Hallet's in London. Hold them up to the light, compare them.

Lucinda holds the lenses up to light, in small lace handkerchief.

LUCINDA

The London – this one? – is quite yellow . . . and this . . . oh, it's so clear! It is lovely.

HASSET

Clear enough for optical lenses.

As he adds more samples to the ones already on his desk, amongst the tea-cups and pamphlets on glass:

That is poison blue, made by the addition of lead oxide.

LUCINDA

And this?

HASSET

A melted lump of beer glass. It is the image of my Bishop.

Lucinda laughs as she holds up the brown glass to discover the face.

He does not like me.

LUCINDA

I can see that in his expression.

HASSET

And now –

Hasset holds up a Prince Rupert's drop.

The pièce-de-résistance.

Lucinda sees the pliers he holds in his other hand.

LUCINDA

No. You must not.

Hasset surprised to find himself peeved.

HASSET

Why must I not?

LUCINDA

Because you know what will happen. When it is gone . . .
Oh.

Lucinda has seen his bad temper.

HASSET
(*belligerent*)

'Oh'?

LUCINDA

I am sorry.

He carefully places the drop and pliers on his desk.

HASSET

There is nothing to be sorry for.

Miffed, he is putting away the glass samples. Lucinda feels quite hot.

LUCINDA

The glassworks that are for sale in Darling Harbour. I wish
to buy them.

Hasset's sulk evaporates in surprise:

HASSET

To buy?

LUCINDA

Will you help me?

HASSET

But I have no knowledge of the commercial side. My theory
is adequate, of course, but I –

Frazer has opened the door, interrupting.

I will be there in a minute, Frazer.

Lucinda stands.

Don't worry about him. No, stay, please. Soon, though, I
have clergyman's business to attend to.

LUCINDA

You cannot help me.

HASSET

On the contrary. Of course I will help you buy your
glassworks.

LUCINDA

I have more than ten thousand pounds.

*Lucinda almost apologetic to have so much. But Hasset, astonished,
has tossed the piece of glass cullet up into the air and caught it:*

HASSET

The deuce you do!

LUCINDA

Will you take the plunge with me?

Lucinda holding out her hand to shake. After a second's pause at this male gesture, Hasset shakes her hand: a deal.

HASSET

Monsieur Leplastrier.

INT. GLASSWORKS. SYDNEY. 1865. DAY

In the cavernous, neglected glassworks Lucinda carries a stack of account books and ledgers. Beside her, Dennis Hasset carries a crate of dusty glass samples. Their echoing voices and footsteps:

HASSET

We shall co-opt, of course. I have a friend, a very clever chap called Wilson. I wish you would let me carry those.

LUCINDA

They are nothing. I have worked on a farm, you know.

Hasset gives her an amused look and sees, indeed, they are nothing to her and realizes, also, that he has to hurry to keep up with her long, unselfconscious stride, made easy by her bloomer costume.

And there is my accountant, Mr d'Abbs.

HASSET

We shall have them both on board. London, of course, is where you should go.

LUCINDA

I have only just arrived here.

HASSET

To buy the very latest machinery. That will make Sydney sit up.

INT. LUCINDA'S ROOM. PETTY'S HOTEL. SYDNEY. 1865. MORNING

In morning light: the glass collection from the farmhouse shines in recognizable little group on the table under the window. Around the room: stacks of ledgers, some open, and glass samples from the glassworks grouped by colour and style: evidence of Lucinda's learning her business.

Lucinda on her way out, passes a young maid with a pile of linen in her arms:

LUCINDA

Leave the glass samples, please, Kate.

KATE

Just left out miss, like that?

The maid quite in awe of this independent young woman.

INT. LOBBY. PETTY'S HOTEL. SYDNEY. 1865. MORNING

Dennis Hasset, in his perfect clerical black, waits in the lobby. He bows, almost in unison, to two elderly gentlemen across the lobby:

NARRATOR
(*voice-over*)

Dennis Hasset knew his behaviour was reckless. His diary recorded the first meeting with Lucinda and after that, many red slashes across previous appointments, even one vestry meeting.

Hasset looks up to see Lucinda hurrying down the stairs, putting on her hat.

As she arrives at the foot of the stairs, she stops on the last step and stretches out one foot:

LUCINDA

You were right in your choice of the tan.

Hasset looks down at Lucinda's foot, in a new tan boot, her ankle exposed, turning this way and that. He can't take his eyes off the neat boot, yet wishes to be looking anywhere but here:

HASSET

Excellent.

As Lucinda and Hasset cross the lobby to leave, he sees two young women from his congregation are watching them.

Sydney got ready to be scandalized.

INT. JIMMY D'ABBS'S HOUSE. RUSHCUTTERS' BAY. NSW. 1865.
NIGHT

NARRATOR
(*voice-over*)

It could not tolerate to see the two of them together. Let her
socialize with Charlie Fig if she wished, or with her
accountant Jimmy d'Abbs.

*Two o'clock in the morning: lamplight falls on the grey blanket covering
the table where cribbage is being played. In the shadows beyond,
paintings hang four deep on the walls.*

French-doors open to summer night.

*Jimmy d'Abbs – a smallish man of forty dressed in an expensive
bohemian style – likes Lucinda's laughter, her pluck, her recklessness.
He gathers in cards, as:*

D'ABBS
Harvey Briggs has bought himself a steamer.

MISS SHADDOCK
He can take us up to Pittwater.

MISS MALCOLM
Or across to Mossman's Bay.

FIG
Who would trust Briggsie with a steamer?

MISS SHADDOCK
I would rather Pittwater.

D'ABBS
We could take her out for the day. Look at this. Two weeks
ago she spilled them everywhere.

Lucinda expertly shuffling cards. Miss Malcolm yawns:

FIG

Have you had enough of cards?

LUCINDA

Oh, please, one more hand.

MISS MALCOLM

You have already lost three guineas. And it is after two o'clock.

D'ABBS

One more hand.

FIG

Now, d'Abbs, you are meant to be looking after the girl's money, not trying to take it from her.

D'ABBS
(*pleased*)

She is free to leave, Fig.

As Lucinda deals a card across the table to Miss Shaddock: it slides across its fellows, sails through the air; Miss Shaddock puts up a hand, it flies back to Lucinda, bounces and falls to the floor.

MISS SHADDOCK

Misdeal!

Lucinda leans down to pick it up, twisting away so she does not see the card.

MISS MALCOLM

I am going to call it a night.

D'ABBS

We have not gone twice around.

What Lucinda does see is: Mr Fig's foot, boot off, up amongst Miss Malcolm's skirts. Lucinda, intent on gambling, blinks, then ignores it:

LUCINDA

Just this one more.

D'ABBS

A duck to water. She has caught the bug.

Lucinda deals, drunk with the game. She only wants more of it. She knows she can control the cards with the strength of her will. Fig's mock finger-wagging:

FIG

We are corrupting you.

EXT. DOG PIT. NOTTING HILL. LONDON. 1869. DAY

The sound of Sunday church bells, in early morning. In crowd of working men: Oscar wearing shabby clerical black for the first time, stands next to man with little terrier tucked under his arm.

The terrier, wearing a woman's bracelet for a collar, stares up into Oscar's face.

TINY'S OWNER

This is Tiny. Say hullo to the Reverend, Tiny.

Tiny holds out a paw. Oscar shakes it.

OSCAR

Hullo, Tiny.

A man is calling the odds in a close crowd of men and dogs sitting on benches around a pit: the centre painted a bright white.

Two men, each holding their dog by the collar, wait in the ring.

The clock is started, the dogs let loose.

INT. VICARAGE. SYDNEY. 1866. DAY

Frazer hangs Lucinda's cape as she hurries away from him into Hasset's study.

She holds up legal documents:

LUCINDA

I have signed! I own the glassworks.

But Hasset is abstracted:

HASSET

My congratulations.

LUCINDA

I must confess to feeling scared.

Lucinda feels his mood: one of tension and misery. She takes in the room: no fire, light darkening outside, cold. Her mood drops. She watches Hasset pouring two sherries.

She takes her glass, raises it, ready for his toast, but instead:

HASSET

I broke with my friend Tom Wilson this afternoon.

LUCINDA

Why is that?

HASSET

He said things about you that are scurrilous.

Lucinda blushes.

LUCINDA

What things?

HASSET

That you stay up all night gambling with Jimmy d'Abbs and Harvey Fig and others of that type.

Lucinda silent.

I told Wilson such stories are pure fabrication, that they should not be repeated. I told him that d'Abbs is your accountant, that you did go to see him, that indeed I went with you.

Lucinda still silent: blushing, tense.

There is no more to it, is there?

LUCINDA

I am sorry you argued with your friend.

She sees his misery, wishes she could assure him.

HASSET

Is there any truth in his story?

LUCINDA

I have been to Mr d'Abbs's house.

HASSET

But, gambling?

LUCINDA

I was lonely.

HASSET

But you have been here three or four nights each week.

Lucinda drinks some sherry.

Wilson mentioned gambling parties on a boat at Pittwater.
And dancing. Not once or twice.

Lucinda raises her glass, distracted.

LUCINDA

There was no dancing. Well, I must go.

She had no idea she was going to say that.

HASSET

But you came to celebrate.

LUCINDA
(*yawns*)

I am too sleepy.

She is eager – even desperate – to escape now.

HASSET

We are having beef.

LUCINDA

I have to meet Mr Queale.

HASSET

At this hour?

LUCINDA

There is still one paper to sign.

HASSET

His office will be closed.

45

We are to meet at Petty's Hotel.

How easy it is to lie. She finishes her sherry. She looks heated, distracted.

I am sorry about your friend.

But she is already at the door.

INT. D'ABBS'S HOUSE. RUSHCUTTERS' BAY. 1866. NIGHT

A card game in progress on the grey-blanketed walnut table.

Lucinda hurries across the room towards the game, flames of hair escape from pins.

They welcome her as Mr d'Abbs pulls out a chair, Fig shuffles cards.

Lucinda opens her purse and tips it upside-down.

LUCINDA
Let me raise the stakes.

Coins fall to the table in a pile, notes float down.

Fig whistles.

Lucinda looks around the table and, as she joins the game:

NARRATOR
(*voice-over*)
Lucinda had an immense feeling of relief – no responsibility, no choice – every loss was one brick less in the foundation of her fortune.

INT. SCHOOL. NOTTING HILL. LONDON. 1869. DAY

A group of schoolboys crowding through the entrance hall, leaving school for sport, with a teacher. The schoolboys part to let Oscar and Fish through.

Both now twenty-eight and wearing clerical clothes: Fish's gleaming, perfect; Oscar's shabby.

As they walk through the poorish school: down corridors, past classrooms and dining-room, with the hum of a school after hours: a small choir practising, boy shouting, a master's voice, clatter of feet up and down stairs.

OSCAR

I went this afternoon to the Church Missionary Society.

FISH

Slow down, Odd Bod.

OSCAR

They will have me if I wish.

FISH

For what?

OSCAR

I enquired about New South Wales.

FISH

There is no need to frighten yourself with such ideas.

As they climb narrow stairs to attic:

OSCAR

Look at me, Fish. I have changed. Look at what I have become.

FISH

Oh, strike me. What have you become?

And they go into:

INT. SCHOOL. NOTTING HILL. LONDON. 1869. DAY

Oscar's little third-floor attic room, cold, with no fire. Neat row of sixteen black clothbound notebooks – Oscar's racetrack system – descendants of the first notebook we saw at Oxford, on a little table.

OSCAR

I have become vile.

FISH

You are not vile. It is just that you do not fit.

47

48

OSCAR

Speak quietly.

FISH

You are perfectly unique.

OSCAR

Do you 'fit'?

FISH

Me? Oh, I 'fit'. I daresay I 'fit' all too well. Look at me. I
am about to marry a Bishop's daughter. You cannot 'fit'
more than that.

*Fish sits in only chair, while Oscar perches on bed. Fish has trouble
lighting his cigar.*

OSCAR

The school pays for all my needs, but I cannot stop gambling.

FISH

But you give it all away. You do not even have coal for a fire.
Look at how you live. You have nothing. Look at your togs.
And stop fidgeting.

OSCAR

I have sunk so low, I gamble even on the Sabbath. On
whatever is going.

Fish leans across to hold Oscar's wrist.

FISH

You do not have to go to New South Wales for penance.

He leans back, re-lights cigar.

And anyway, you cannot.

Oscar smiles, waving away blue smoke.

OSCAR

Why not?

FISH
(*sunny*)

Because you cannot bear a little aqua. You could not sail as
far as Calais.

But Oscar is pushing a florin across the little table – with notebooks on it – towards Fish, who picks it up and puts it down.

You wish me to flip this?

OSCAR

Yes.

FISH

You know I only flip my own coins.

He eventually finds a penny.

He flips – almost lethargically – as if the coin isn't to decide his friend's destiny.

Penny spins through the air.

Call.

Oscar pale and waxy.

The penny lands in Fish's palm, his fingers close over it.

Call.

Fish flips it on to the back of his hand, covered.

OSCAR

I cannot.

FISH

Why not?

OSCAR

You know I am frightened.

FISH

Then why do such things to yourself? Come, dear Odd Bod, and –

OSCAR
(*over*)

Heads.

Fish sighs. Lifts his hand to reveal:

The head of Queen Victoria.

Oscar's face ghastly.

EXT. DOCKS. LEVIATHAN. SOUTHAMPTON. 1869. DAY

Sound of the busy docks. As we travel down the wet docks, past the high walls of the ship, we see a cow in a sling, being winched up, up in the air, all dangling legs, stretched neck and mournful bellow. It passes the giant letters: LEVIATHAN *painted on the metal side of the huge ship:*

> NARRATOR
> (*voice-over*)
> For a man who could not bear a little aqua, the *Leviathan* was the only ship to travel on. In second class you could go eight weeks and never find your way to a porthole with a view of the sea.

We travel on, up the high side of the ship, with the cow in the sling, to the sound of the steam crane winching it up, and come to a stack of crates, on the deck, stamped with the letters: PRINCE RUPERT'S GLASSWORKS SYDNEY AUSTRALIA

The cow is lowered into a hold.

The owner of the Prince Rupert's Glassworks.

EXT. DOCKS. LEVIATHAN. SOUTHAMPTON. 1869. DAY

The Captain on the bridge with a little group of first-class passengers: a Belgian family with two little dogs. Lucinda leaning on the rails to see if there is another cow to be winched up:

> NARRATOR
> (*voice-over*)
> had been told that on a clear day you could see all the way to China from first class.

To her amazement, a cage swings into view:

It pauses, swaying for a moment, almost at eye level. In it are Oscar, blindfolded, green-faced, squatting between Hugh Stratton, who holds his arms from behind, and Wardley-Fish.

OSCAR
Are we almost there, Fish?

Lucinda's gaze follows the cage's swaying, jerking progress as it is winched higher.

INT. LEVIATHAN. 1869. DAY

The second-class promenade, where stewards move among the passengers and their guests.

A little group of people, including schoolboys and a teacher, gathered around Oscar, Wardley-Fish, the Strattons and Theophilus.

Theophilus watches Oscar, in the group of schoolboys and his few friends. Although Theophilus and Oscar have met only three painful times since Oscar left home, his son is beautiful to him, reminding him of his wife. Theophilus holds, clasped with his Bible, a little tin case.

Hugh and Betty, each with sherry glass and cake, stand on either side of Theophilus.

BETTY
Goodness, what a splurge all this is –

HUGH

Is it you who have paid the boy's passage?

Now Theophilus takes his eyes off Oscar, for a second, to look at Hugh:

THEOPHILUS

I would not have him go away.

HUGH

It is certainly not the Missionary Society.

From this group on the second-class promenade Melody, Fish's fiancée, sees Lucinda watching from the threshold of the velvet curtains which divides second-class from the first-class salon.

Melody is almost sick with embarrassment to be part of this odd group. She is horrified when Theophilus drops to his knees.

MELODY

Oh, dearest, stop him.

But Fish looks away.

A steward has moved, not understanding, to help Theophilus up. But stops as Oscar kneels beside his father.

Melody mortified to see her fiancé aping the Evangelicals, leans down, whispering:

Get up. You are not one of them.

But now everyone is kneeling: Hugh and Betty Stratton, schoolboys, their teacher, even strangers.

Only the stewards remain standing, but even they bow their heads, fold their hands. What can Melody do? She kneels.

Lucinda, at the first-class curtain, can't take her eyes off this oddly appealing spectacle. Megaphone blaring from outside only accentuates the deep, listening quietness.

THEOPHILUS

O, Lord God.

Theophilus's voice tangled with emotion, with the love he has for his son. He starts again:

Oh, Lord God. This is my son . . . from whom I have been estranged.

Another painful pause in the silence.

These are his friends and fellow voyagers. Oh, Lord. What can we do?

A silence. People continue to kneel, heads bowed.

But Theophilus is on his feet. Holding out a little tissue-wrapped fragment to Oscar:

Here. It is your caul. From off your little head, when you were born. It is said to save you from drowning.

As Oscar takes his caul:

Will we never stand together, beside God, on that Happy Day?

But his voice is a stranger in his throat and, with a touch so light Oscar wonders if he has imagined it, his father leaves.

As Theophilus walks quickly away, the congregation rises slowly, not keen to meet each other's eyes.

INT. LEVIATHAN. 1869. DAY

The Purser's Assistant ringing a bell, calling for All Visitors Ashore as Hugh Stratton runs down the stairs past him and past two visitors hurrying upstairs.

Oscar, sitting on chaise-longue in promenade, is examining the little case his father left for him: 'O. J. P. Hopkins, a gift from his father' engraved on the lid.

Oscar takes the tissue-wrapped caul out of his pocket and puts it inside the little case, which holds a set of soldering implements with hand-made wooden handles.

Hugh, running up behind Oscar, startles him.

>   HUGH
> You can no longer put me off.

Hugh sits beside Oscar, picking up a discarded half-glass of sherry:

> There has been too much cat and mouse.

He gulps his sherry.

> We did not think we were educating a wealthy man.

Hugh looks around the luxurious promenade. Sirens blasting.

>   OSCAR
> I am not a wealthy —

Hugh takes Oscar's wrist, squeezes it, keeps it gripped.

>   HUGH
>   (over)
> I am not a cadger. I do not come begging. You must tell me how it is you have managed all this.

>   OSCAR
> If I were to tell you and my father heard of it, it would be a torture beyond his toleration —

>   HUGH
>   (over)
> You have my word he never shall.

Oscar still hesitates.

Dear Oscar, accept my word.

> OSCAR

I have gambled.

Hugh lets out a big breath, but does not let go of Oscar.

> HUGH

So. Gambled.

> OSCAR

The ship is moving.

> HUGH

You have a system. Is that what it is called?

> OSCAR

A system?

> HUGH

You have a system and you will write it down for me.

Old envelope, stubby pencil being thrust one-handed at Oscar.

OSCAR

It is not a simple thing you can just write down. We have
left it too late.

Hugh's face goes slack, helpless. His grip loosens.

HUGH

Write it down, boy, please, I beg of you.

OSCAR

You must go.

HUGH

Is it horses?

OSCAR

It is.

Hugh lets go of Oscar's wrist.

The sirens blasting their final warning.

HUGH

You swear before God you will send me your system?

OSCAR

I do.

Hugh nods. Sirens continue to blast.

*Oscar watches Hugh as he runs along the promenade, one hand
clutching his sciatic back.*

*Oscar alone on chaise-longue in deserted promenade rubs his wrist
where Hugh has squeezed it. The faintest of sounds from the deck.*

INT. LEVIATHAN. 1869. DAY

*Five stewards playing cards in empty stateroom, furniture dust-sheeted.
The intensity and camaraderie of the game.*

Smoke hangs in the air, floating up to ventilation grille.

INT. LUCINDA'S CABIN. LEVIATHAN. 1869. DAY

Lucinda stands on tiptoe at ventilation grille in her cabin, listening to the tantalizing words of the stewards' card game. The voices make her desperate to play.

She walks about her cabin, the voices only a murmur now. She puts a pack of cards into a small velvet purse.

INT. LEVIATHAN. 1869. DAY

Lucinda running up narrow metal steps.

She comes to two doors. She does a quick:

                    LUCINDA
    . . . eeny meeny miney mo . . .

And ends on the right-hand door, which she opens to:

INT. LEVIATHAN. 1869. DAY

Oscar, sitting on his chaise-longue, looking straight at Lucinda in the doorway.

Lucinda feels that her search for a card game must be clear, that her guilt is visible. She feels caught in the act. But, rather than turn back, she pretends it was Oscar, and not a card game, she is searching for.

Oscar watches Lucinda as, chin up, she crosses to him.

They look at each other, neither quite listening to the automatic words as they introduce themselves.

                    LUCINDA
    Lucinda Leplastrier. How do you do?

                    OSCAR
    Oscar Hopkins. How do you do?

                    LUCINDA
    Do you hear confession?

                    OSCAR
    I have done.

LUCINDA

Would you hear mine?

OSCAR

Of course.

LUCINDA

Thank you.

Lucinda bows her blushing face and flees.

OSCAR

Where shall I find you?

LUCINDA

I am in first class.

Oscar watches Lucinda hurrying away.

INT. LEVIATHAN. 1869. NIGHT

Oscar, in ship's corridor, comes to the foot of a staircase. He is sick with fear. He pauses, feels in his pocket, and takes out the little tissue-wrapped caul his father gave him. Silently prays to God to keep him safe. Puts the caul back, and starts on his ascent to Lucinda's first-class cabin:

NARRATOR
(*voice-over*)

In order that I exist, two gamblers, one obsessive, the other compulsive, must declare themselves.

INT. LEVIATHAN. 1869. NIGHT

Lucinda's itchy desire to gamble as she shuffles cards at the table. A knock on the door.

Lucinda opens the door to: a sweating Oscar with his Prayer Book clasped to his chest. Lucinda doesn't know why Oscar is here. She only knows he must not see the cards and money on the table.

OSCAR

You must excuse me for not coming earlier.

As Lucinda goes towards the windows, away from cards on table:

59

LUCINDA

Of course. You must come and look at my view. The Purser
calls them 'landscape' windows but I argued they should
be called 'seascape' –

Lucinda realizes Oscar has not followed her.

*Instead, he has turned away, his back to windows, and is moving
awkwardly, directly to the table, as if to a life-buoy.*

Oscar makes the table and, relieved, sits with his back to the windows.

*Lucinda stays standing so Oscar has to look up at her, rather than at
the cards and money. Is it possible he has not noticed them?*

OSCAR

You see, I have a phobia about the ocean.

LUCINDA
(*distracted*)

I see.

*But all she can see is that Oscar has picked up a card and is fiddling
with it, although not looking at it.*

OSCAR

My father was a naturalist and was in the ocean all the time.
I, too, when I was a little chap.

*It is like having Spanish spoken when she expected to hear Greek.
She tries not to look at the card in his hand.*

But I developed a nervousness about it, like some have with
heights. So, to come up here with all this glass, to hear your
confession, well, I feared it was more than I could manage.

Lucinda now remembers her blurted request for confession.

But I owe you an apology. As you see, I was capable of
coming all the time.

*Oscar has opened his tiny Prayer Book. Lucinda in a panic. She does
not want to confess to Oscar.*

*She looks at his beautifully shaped hands, his flaming hair, his fine
face. Her throat dry. She sits.*

The Lord be in thy heart and on thy lips and give thee grace to make a true and faithful confession.

Lucinda can't speak. Oscar looks up at her, waiting.

She looks into his green eyes.

Then, head bowed, she speaks so quietly he has to lean forward to hear her.

> LUCINDA
>
> I confess to God Almighty, and the whole company of Heaven, and to you, that I have sinned. I have attended rooms in Drury Lane for the purpose of playing fan-tan. I have played dice on a train full of racing types. I did not attend the racetrack but went on that train expressly to play dice. I tried to persuade a business colleague of mine to take me to a cockfight. He refused, but I would have gone. I set up the table, here, like this, as a trap for the stewards, who I know to play poker. I wished to play with them.

Oscar's head also bowed now. His heart beating wildly. Oscar groans. His hands clenched into fists.

Lucinda doesn't dare to look up at him. She waits for the words of absolution.

A long silence.

> OSCAR
>
> The dice you played on the train, was it Dutch Hazards?

Lucinda looks up sharply, but Oscar's head still bent.

> LUCINDA
>
> Yes, it was. We also played another game.

> OSCAR
>
> Old British, perhaps?

Lucinda feels a blush rising. Her feelings unfocused.

> LUCINDA
>
> In New South Wales it's known as Seventh Man.

Oscar feels a reckless joy rising in him.

OSCAR

And who provided the Peter?

He unclenches his hands, places them on the table. Lucinda looks at Oscar's almost blank face.

LUCINDA

The Peter?

OSCAR

Is the term unknown to you?

LUCINDA
(carefully)

No. I think it is quite familiar.

Oscar closes Prayer Book. It goes into his pocket.

OSCAR

I thought so.

LUCINDA

These terms, Mr Hopkins, are they also familiar to you?

Oscar's smile is clear and brilliant.

OSCAR

I am afraid so.

Lucinda smiles, with less certainty.

LUCINDA

This is most improper.

Oscar, now very pleased, wipes his brow and hands with handkerchief, as:

OSCAR

I don't think so.

LUCINDA

You have not absolved me.

OSCAR

Where is the sin?

Lucinda is shocked. Not only by his words but by the sudden change of mood, into dangerous lightness.

Our whole faith is a wager. We bet – it is all in Pascal, you know – we bet that there is a God. We bet our life on it. We calculate the odds, the return, that we shall sit with the saints in paradise. Our anxiety about our bet wakes us before dawn in a cold sweat. And God sees us suffer. I cannot see that such a God, whose fundamental requirement of us is that we gamble our mortal souls – it is true! We stake everything on the fact of His existence –

Lucinda sees not only Oscar's passion for salvation but his fear of damnation. It is a mirror she looks into, and a window. Oscar's hands sweep across table, gathering cards:

– that such a God can look unkindly on a chap wagering a few quid on the likelihood of a dumb animal crossing the line first, unless –

And now he is shuffling cards, smiling at Lucinda.

– unless it might be considered a blasphemy to apply to common pleasure that which is divine.

Oscar holds up the pack of cards:

Shall we play?

How can Lucinda resist?

INT. LEVIATHAN. 1869. NIGHT

Lucinda's bed-coverings pulled back.

A blanket from her bed covers the table, lit by a lamp.

Lucinda and Oscar in intense concentration of poker game.

A hand finished. Lucinda shuffles cards.

LUCINDA
What a surprise.

OSCAR
What a turn-up for the books.

She looks at Oscar and laughs. Oscar looks at her beautiful laugh and smiles with pleasure.

INT. LEVIATHAN. 1869. NIGHT

Lucinda's hat-box slides along its shelf.

The ship makes creaking, cracking noises as it enters a long, deep swell.

The game has changed. No longer a concentrated stillness. Lucinda leans forward. Oscar's leg jiggles, foot taps. Oscar wins. Lucinda raises the betting: light, almost giddy with reckless pleasure. The ship's movement more pronounced.

A vase of paper flowers slides off shelf and rolls along floor. Lucinda's hat-box tumbles from its shelf.

Oscar turns – involuntarily, as Lucinda turns – to see:

White head of wave filling portholes.

Oscar cries out. Lucinda turns to see him white-faced with terror.

Oscar crouches over table, trying to pick up cards, like a savage, making a continuous high moaning noise.

The sound and solid weight of waves crashing against ship.

Oscar crumpling cards as he shoves them into his pockets.

OSCAR

I have led you astray.

Sounds of ship groaning, creaking, doors banging, the ship's bells ringing.

You must forgive me.

Lucinda has to shout.

LUCINDA

Yes, yes, of course I forgive you.

The ship rears, rolls sideways. Oscar battles up the incline towards the portholes.

OSCAR

I played for pleasure.

He is at the portholes. Winding one open, facing the terror of the world of violent water outside.

No!

He feeds the cards out of the little gap he has made.

Lucinda pulls at his hands but she saves only two cards.

Oscar turns, clutches at Lucinda. Frightened, she steps back.

Oscar falls to the floor, fainting. Water hisses through the open porthole.

INT. LEVIATHAN. 1869. DAY

Just before dawn, the ship still pitching and rolling. Oscar's half-conscious body is being carried out of Lucinda's stateroom, and down the corridor, by two stewards.

INT. LEVIATHAN. 1869. DAY

Lucinda plays patience at her table. A luncheon tray, the food half-finished, beside her.

Clear southern-hemisphere light through porthole.

NARRATOR
(*voice-over*)
The scandal kept Lucinda a prisoner in her stateroom. She waited for Oscar to apologize, but she did not hear a word.

INT. LEVIATHAN. 1869. DAY

Oscar, green and sick, in bed. A steward props him up, gently feeding him beef tea: a Nurse with a baby.

NARRATOR
(*voice-over*)
My great-grandfather did not emerge from his cabin until the Pinchgut cannons saluted the great ship's entry into Sydney Harbour.

INT. LEVIATHAN. 1869. DAY

The Leviathan docked. The second-class passengers, including Oscar, being kept waiting on deck by stewards, as:

The first-class passengers – the Belgian family with their little dogs, followed by Lucinda – are shepherded towards the gangplank.

Lucinda happens to glance at the waiting passengers. She sees Oscar.

Oscar smiles at Lucinda, raises a hand.

She cuts him.

INT. VICARAGE. SYDNEY. 1869. DAY

Hasset's study is almost unrecognizable: the room dismantled, wooden packing crates in process of being filled. A skew of papers and letters on the floor, a crate filled with torn and crumpled papers, no chairs to sit on.

Lucinda and Hasset face each other on packing cases. The room is cold and Lucinda keeps on her rabbitskin coat.

> LUCINDA
>
> But surely you can appeal?

Hasset shakes his head, no. Lucinda wishes he would sit up straighter on his packing case.

> Then damn him.

She is almost crying. He leans across and puts his hand over hers. But Lucinda's tears are for herself. She does not want her hand held and uses the excuse of a handkerchief to remove it.

> Where is Boat Harbour? Is it far away?

> HASSET
>
> Far enough. It is the territory of the Kumbaingiri tribe. What does 'far' mean in this country?

> LUCINDA
>
> I will no longer have my adviser.

Her softness affects him.

> HASSET
>
> I will never forget how you came in here to learn about glass, do you remember? I thought you a Monsieur Leplastrier. What a to-do we caused.

LUCINDA

Were we improper?

HASSET

A degree or two hotter than that.

Lucinda smiles but she feels an uneasy new thought:

LUCINDA

And we were noted?

HASSET
(*grins*)

They could not help themselves.

LUCINDA

Then I am responsible for your exile.

HASSET
(*over*)

No –

LUCINDA

Yes, and you've tried to hide it from me. I never –

HASSET
(*over*)

Hush.

LUCINDA

I never thought.

HASSET
(*over*)

Hush. Do you hear me? You are wrong. Quite wrong. Now,
please. It is wholly theological.

LUCINDA

You are not forced to go.

Lucinda stands to turn on a lamp.

HASSET

I have no choice. I must go where I am sent.

LUCINDA

By God?

HASSET

Of course.

LUCINDA

Or a man, a bishop?

HASSET

Oh, please, do leave it alone.

She sits again, opposite him, on the packing case:

LUCINDA

What will happen to you in a place where there is nothing but mud and taverns and no church?

HASSET

No church building.

LUCINDA

Stay. Please. We can have the works together.

She knows she begs. She watches him consider it.

HASSET

And neither of us lonely.

They look at each other. Sound from hallway briefly of Frazer's voice does not break the deeper silence, which grows almost unbearable, until:

I must go.

LUCINDA

So you will preach what you do not believe to men who do not care.

HASSET

I will preach what I do believe.

LUCINDA

That there is no Virgin birth?

HASSET

That Christ died for our sins that we might be redeemed through His blood, that we might sit at the side of God in Heaven.

Lucinda surprised, even impressed, by the passion, never heard before, in his voice.

LUCINDA

So there is a part of you that wishes to be sent away?

HASSET

Quite a large part.

Lucinda barely aware of herself, one glove on, the other off, turns over books in an open crate. She feels humiliated and does not understand why she has been rejected.

LUCINDA

Who will I have to talk to?

EXT. DEAN'S HOUSE. SYDNEY. 1869. DAY

Light so bright it makes Oscar squint, on this cold winter day. Wind blows up the narrow crooked Sydney streets and makes people hold on to their hats, skirts blow around legs.

Oscar stops to watch an Aboriginal busker who sings an Irish song. He drops a penny into the man's hat. The sound of the voice follows him as he checks he is at the right house. As he does, Dennis Hasset passes him to go inside.

INT. DEAN'S HOUSE. SYDNEY. 1869. DAY

Bishop Dancer stands at the head of the Dean's dinner table, gripping the corners of the damask tablecloth in either hand.

Oscar, Dennis Hasset, the Dean, another vicar, and two rich parishioners at the table: all men, the women have left them to port.

BISHOP

Do not fear for your wife's cloth, Dean.

DEAN

My Lord –

BISHOP

Not a drop will spill. You will see I was not boasting. I will take a small bet on it.

70

They all demur, showing their confidence in the Bishop. Oscar looks down, not to be tempted.

Will no one humour me?

PARISHIONER

Half-a-crown, My Lord, double or nothing.

BISHOP

Done.

As the Dean slyly removes the port decanter to the floor and all the men hold their glasses:

Now, concentrate, watch. You will not see this done by many other Bishops.

The Bishop tests the tension of the tablecloth.

Oscar stands, impulsively, leans across to gravy boat: all elbows and knees.

OSCAR

Allow me to remove this.

BISHOP

Sit down!

Oscar sits.

The Bishop takes more pressure on the cloth, pulls, increasing the tension to the point of movement.

Then swiftly, deftly, he pulls the cloth right off the table. A matador, a cry of triumph.

Everything settles back on to the polished cedar, except:

The gravy boat flies off the table to smash on the floor.

There. You did not believe I could do it.

He is right but they all demur, as they stand, relieved the show is over.

The Bishop hands the tablecloth to Hasset to fold.

Below them, Oscar crouches on the floor, collecting the pieces of broken gravy-boat.

I hear that your Glass Lady is returned.

HASSET

I beg your pardon, my Lord?

Oscar, crouched beside the table, he realizes it is Lucinda they talk about:

BISHOP

Your 'petite amie'.

HASSET

Miss Leplastrier is not that, my Lord.

BISHOP

You will just have time for your farewells before you are off.

As Oscar stands, holding pieces of broken china:

HASSET

I am told it is called the Parish of Never-Never.

BISHOP

Our last chap was run out of town. Never-never come back they told him.

The Bishop laughs.

Oscar stares at Hasset: is he Lucinda's beloved?

Hasset puts the folded tablecloth on to the table.

Oscar places the little pile of broken china on the cloth.

INT. ST JOHN'S VICARAGE. SYDNEY. 1869. DAY

Oscar, wearing a plain black cassock, sits at his desk trying to concentrate on writing a sermon. He is distracted by the sound of a crowd's roaring and cheering, of horses drumming on the track, carrying into his study.

He puts down his pen. He feels tortured, listening to the intoxicating, forbidden sound. He covers his ears.

Mrs Judd, burly, rough and rich, a devoted parishioner, his housekeeper, comes into Oscar's study carrying pristine vestments.

Oscar covers his ears.

She comes around in front of him. He uncovers his ears:

MRS JUDD
Does the track bother you, sir?

OSCAR
A little, Mrs Judd.

MRS JUDD
You grow accustomed to it, in time.

As Mrs Judd carefully places the vestments across an armchair, we go up to Oscar's window and look out to see:

Smack-bang next door is the racetrack: a partial view shows horses, vivid jockeys' colours, flashing past down the home stretch. The crowd's noise rises.

EXT. TREVIS FARM. BELLINGER RIVER. NSW. 1869. DAY

Light falls on a stretch of Bellinger River where it sweeps around from the Harbour promontory. We see it from a high – unseen – point of view.

Into this view comes: a barge with a still figure, dressed in black, on it.

EXT. BELLINGER RIVER. NSW. 1869. DAY

Dennis Hasset – impeccably dressed in vicar's black – sits on the barge, surrounded by his crates. Two men in wide straw hats pole the barge. A gentleman arrives in Boat Harbour.

EXT. TREVIS FARM. BELLINGER RIVER. NSW. 1869. DAY

We discover the high point of view is that of beautiful, dark-haired governess Miriam Chadwick.

She stands – dressed in deep mourning – with eye-glasses held up, to watch the arrival of the barge. Miriam lowers the glasses.

Two children – a little boy and a girl – sit at verandah table doing schoolwork.

I cannot find Paraguay, Mrs Chadwick.

As Miriam hurries past the children, into the house, her footsteps sharp and business-like on the wooden verandah, she is undoing her bodice.

MIRIAM
Have you looked in the index, Alice?

INT. TREVIS FARM. BELLINGER RIVER. NSW. 1869. DAY

Miriam's boots trample her skirt off and kick it aside, as she hurries to wardrobe. She opens the door to reveal a row of mourning clothes: everything scrupulously black.

Miriam's hands part the clothes, to draw from its hiding-place at the back of the wardrobe: an aqua, moiré-silk riding-habit.

Her pleased assessment as she swiftly holds it against herself.

INT. STAIRCASE. MEETING ROOM. BOAT HARBOUR. NSW. 1869. DAY

Miriam, in aqua riding costume, runs up narrow stairs. She carries a bunch of flowers.

INT. MEETING ROOMS. BOAT HARBOUR. NSW. 1869. DAY

The meeting room, set up as a church: a table with a cross on the wall behind it, a few rows of wooden chairs.

The Verger, Mary and two older church women – one of them Mary's mother – are charmed by Hasset:

VERGER
I am sorry we have no better a place for service –

HASSET
Why be sorry, Verger? Wherever we gather – isn't it true? – God is with us, in a cathedral or under a tree, as with our first settlers –

MARY'S MOTHER
Our Lord was born in a stable, Verger.

But they are interrupted by the sound of hurrying footsteps and the vision of Miriam – breathless, with flowers – coming into the room:

MIRIAM
I have brought flowers for the altar.

She doesn't have to look directly at Dennis Hasset to know the effect of her flushed beauty.

EXT. LUCINDA'S HOUSE. LONG NOSE POINT. SYDNEY. 1869. NIGHT

Looking down to where lights shine in windows of Lucinda's isolated house, on the rocky ridge of Long Nose Point, surrounded by harbour.

NARRATOR
(*voice-over*)
Lucinda's head was burning with dreams of glass.

INT. LUCINDA'S HOUSE. 1869. NIGHT

A detailed, amateurish drawing of a glass pyramid. Another of a glass arcade. Another of a glass tower.

Lucinda's cat sits amongst these drawings – and other half-finished, abandoned follies – on the big table in the sitting-room. Stacks of books on floor and table. Lucinda bent over pages of a letter.

LUCINDA
(*voice-over, writing*)
I am taking drawing lessons from a Monsieur Huille and am attempting to draw what I dream of building. What do you think of a glass arcade to cover George Street or a pyramid for the circular quay? Dear Dennis, I wish you were here to advise me. Are you homesick for Sydney?

She signs her name and folds the dozen pages into a fat rectangle. She has just written Dennis Hasset's name on the envelope, when:

Wind rattles the dark, uncurtained windows.

She looks up. The room's reflection in the glass. A floorboard creaks behind her.

The cat's head comes up, alert.

Lucinda holds her breath, feels her scalp creep.

She will not stay to be frightened, she stands noisily. Turns to face the stranger behind her. No one.

The cat watches as she walks to the door: her boots ringing on the boards.

EXT. ARGYLE CUT. THE ROCKS. SYDNEY. 1869. NIGHT

Lucinda ties her horse and trap to railings outside a shop-front where a candle – burning inside a lantern – stands in the empty window. A few men in twos and threes standing around outside.

INT. CHINESE GAMBLING ROOMS. SYDNEY. 1869. NIGHT

A bright light shines above the zinc-covered fan-tan table. The zinc throws back a glow on to the faces of the gamblers – only men – pressed in hot crowd around the table.

Intense silence as the young Chinese croupier, with gold teeth and pigtail, throws the brass coins.

The coins hit the zinc.

Lucinda pushing through the crowd of men around the table, towards the bright zinc in its pool of light.

The croupier's tin cup hides some of the coins, his right hand sweeps away the rest: all movements deft and elegant. Three fingers ringed, one with emerald. He lifts the cup, slides the coins into sets of four, to mounting tension.

Sound of men barracking all around Lucinda: 'Yes'. 'No'. Groans. A cheer. 'It's two!'

CROUPIER
(*calls*)

Toe. Numma toe.

Croupier gives out the winnings. Crude remarks and laughter in the crowd of men. Lucinda is now almost at the table, at the bright square of pitted zinc.

LUCINDA

Excuse me.

Where Lucinda had felt anonymous, unnoticed, in the hot press of men, now she feels a cool space open around her as they acknowledge her presence. She is no longer lonely, frightened or shy.

Red numerals – 1 2 3 4 – in pitted and scratched paint on the bright square of zinc.

Lucinda places a florin against the four. Men place coppers next to it.

The croupier does his business. The four wins.

INT. CHINESE GAMBLING ROOMS. SYDNEY. 1869. NIGHT

Lucinda feels the men's approval, as well as the familiar electric ecstasy, beyond salvation and uncaring. She looks at no one. She plays with inspired recklessness. She feels she can control the game with her will.

INT. CHINESE GAMBLING ROOMS. SYDNEY. 1869. NIGHT

Three a.m. and Lucinda watches the last of her money being swept across the bright zinc.

She moves away from the table, through the crowd – smaller now –

and as she reaches the edge of the crowd, out of the bright pool of light, she looks in her purse: empty, cleared out. She feels as light and clean as rice-paper.

She notices a portrait of Queen Victoria in the shadows around the wall.

Below it: a familiar face.

Lucinda's confusion. She opens her purse again: pretending to look in it.

She looks up at the face again: the fine eyes, the flaming hair.

Oscar smiles at her.

She snaps her purse shut. Puts it in her bag.

He tosses a coin, catching it on back of his hand.

He stands.

EXT. ST JOHN'S VICARAGE. SYDNEY. 1869. DAWN

Early light of morning.

Mr Judd holds his horse's bridle – Mrs Judd sitting side-saddle – as they both look up the yellow driveway to the vicarage. The Judds are both burly, rough and rich, and devoted to their church. Their worry to see:

The windows unshuttered, lights burning inside.

INT./EXT. ST JOHN'S VICARAGE. SYDNEY. 1869. DAWN

Lucinda gathers her winnings: five pounds in notes and coins. Oscar gathers the cards. A fire burns in the grate, in this genteel, over-furnished room. Lucinda stretches and sticks out her stockinged feet, her shoes lie on the carpet, as they continue their conversation:

LUCINDA
No, Mr Hasset did not ask to go North, he was sent.

OSCAR
I asked and was refused.

The Bishop refused you?

OSCAR

He said God had work for me to do in Randwick. Now I understand why he laughed when I asked if there were any blacks in the congregation.

Oscar smiles in response to Lucinda's laugh.

Mr Judd climbing up on to verandah. Mrs Judd watching from below as Mr Judd heavily tiptoes to windows.

Lucinda neatly folding notes.

LUCINDA

There is not even a church building up there. They use a room above the cobbler's for service.

OSCAR

Is Mr Hasset a good friend?

LUCINDA

A very dear friend.

Lucinda yawns as she puts notes and coins into purse.

Wide-mouthed, she looks up to see, over Oscar's shoulder:

Mr Judd's face – distorted by flawed, yellowish glass and a coin of condensation – looms at the window, like something out of her worst fears.

Erg.

Oscar smiles, puzzled.

She wants to scream.

Oscar is making a bridge: the cards fan out flashing through the air, a moving span between his hands.

Mr Judd beating on the window. Roaring. Mrs Judd climbing with difficulty up on to the verandah behind him.

Oscar jumps and, just as he brings the bridge back to its neat pack, turns to see:

The faces at the window.

Lucinda is taking her hat-pin from her hat, a weapon. She is amazed to see Oscar going to the window.

Oscar unlocks the window. Mr Judd's words through the glass. His indignant mouth.

MR JUDD
I'll tell you this, sir –

As Oscar pushes up window:

OSCAR
Mr Judd. Mrs Judd. Please come in.

Lucinda incredulous. She holds hat-pin behind her back.

The obedient Judds are clambering over the sill and into sitting-room.

Oscar steps back, astonished, nervous, hardly aware he has made the invitation.

Mr Judd has to bend to brush down his indignant wife's disarranged skirts, as:

MR JUDD
You have been gambling.

A cold draft from open window makes everything flutter.

We will not have it, sir.

Mrs Judd keeps Lucinda in her sights: a steady stream of indignant anger.

It is no good denying it.

OSCAR
I am not denying it.

Lucinda moves to pick up her hat.

MRS JUDD
She is slipping out.

OSCAR
I am sorry if I have caused offence.

MRS JUDD

She is putting on her hat.

OSCAR

She is my guest, Mrs Judd.

MRS JUDD

A pretty name for it.

MR JUDD
(*warns*)

Mrs Judd.

MRS JUDD

I'll not be stopped. He is a hypocrite. We make him lovely
vestments. He will not wear them. Isn't that true? You think
God would rather see you looking like a crow.

OSCAR
(*over*)

I wear what –

MR JUDD
(*over*)

You dress like a scarecrow, sir.

MRS JUDD
(*over*)

He dresses like a scarecrow. And throws out our Messiah,
and our candles. And here he is with cards and women in
the temple.

Lucinda steps in to the pause in Mrs Judd's indignation:

LUCINDA

You are a rude woman. And you a rude man. You imagine
you are civilized, but you are like savages with toppers and
tails. You should pray to God to forgive you your rudeness.

Oscar aghast, about to apologize to the Judds:

You may leave.

The Judds, cowed, move uncertainly towards door.

The way you came.

The Judds' awkward backs as they clamber out through the window.

Lucinda calls.

Close it.

The window closed after them.

Lucinda at window, watching the Judds walk away down path, expelled.

Lucinda begins to laugh.

Oscar looks at her face: lovely in its unguarded laughter. He starts to laugh with her.

Then he sits suddenly. Groans. His hands make his hair wild.

OSCAR

I am done for.

LUCINDA

Surely not.

Lucinda looks at Oscar. Then around the vicarage room: at the cards and money on the table and wonders if he could be right.

INT. ANGLICAN VICARAGE. DEVON. 1869. DAY

Oscar's sixteen black clothbound notebooks spread out on the Stratton's dining table. Pages of calculations in Hugh's sprawling handwriting amongst them. Anxious Betty counts out coins onto a pile of notes:

BETTY

. . . and fifteen shillings. That's every penny, Hugh.

HUGH

We will double it –

BETTY

All of my capital.

HUGH

– treble it. His system works. It is foolproof.

BETTY

How can you be sure?

HUGH

The boy has proven it. Dear Betty, have faith.

Hugh has put money into jacket, Betty puts on her hat. The clock strikes eight. Hugh keen to be off. But it is Betty who remembers the pages of calculations.

EXT./INT. HOPKINS'S COTTAGE. DEVON. 1869. DAY

Corals from the ocean, covered with water, laid out in a large flat tray. Theophilus bends over the tray, examining a coral with a lens.

He looks up to see, from window:

Hugh and Betty Stratton making their way along the red-mud path in front of house. Betty with her forward-leaning walk, as if making her way in strong head-wind, with Hugh, whose walk today has a nervous jerky energy to it.

They disappear, leaving only the sky, headland, and wind-blown trees.

Instead of returning to his corals, Theophilus picks up, and worries over, an already often-read letter – starting a few pages in:

OSCAR
(*voice-over letter*)

When I told the Ecclesiastical Commission

INT. BOARDING HOUSE. SYDNEY. 1869. DAY

OSCAR
(*voice-over*)

that I had never gambled for personal gain, they would not believe me. They have cast me out.

Oscar prays, hands locked together, fingernails digging into the knuckles, kneeling in shabby boarding-house room.

INT. HOPKINS'S COTTAGE. DEVON. 1869. DAY

OSCAR
(*voice-over*)

I am sorry to have caused you so much anguish, dear
Papa. I know that you will believe that I am destined for
eternal hellfire.

Theophilus has bowed his head in prayer over Oscar's letter.

EXT. SYDNEY STREETS. NSW. 1869. DAY

Lucinda drives her trap, on a mission:

EXT. ST JOHN'S VICARAGE. SYDNEY. 1869. DAY

OSCAR
(*voice-over*)

It does seem there is nothing for a man to do once he has
gained the reputation that has been so unjustly given to
me.

*The sound of the racetrack from next door as Lucinda draws up at the
front steps of vicarage.*

*She looks up to where Mrs Judd has been sweeping the front verandah
and now stands, holding the broom, as if to defend her temple.*

LUCINDA

Is Mr Hopkins here?

MRS JUDD

No. He is not.

LUCINDA

Would you tell me where he is gone?

MRS JUDD

No. I cannot. I am only a savage.

*Lucinda sees it is hopeless to plead. She flicks her whip and trots away
at fast clip, leaving a cloud of yellow dust to settle on Mrs Judd's
verandah.*

INT. CHINESE GAMBLING ROOMS. SYDNEY. 1869. NIGHT

Rooms crowded with gamblers.

Lucinda walking from the Pak-Ah-Pu room into the more intense atmosphere of the fan-tan room.

She is distracted, looking for Oscar's distinctive hair, fine face, black clothes. He is not here.

EXT. LANEWAY. SYDNEY. 1869. DAY

A small group of men gathered around a two-up game.

Lucinda turns into laneway, coming towards game.

As she passes the game, her eyes go quickly over the group, searching for Oscar, as she always does.

INT. POST OFFICE. SYDNEY. 1869. DAY

Lucinda walking through Post Office with mail to post.

She sees Oscar, his back to her, standing at counter. Here he is, when she had given up looking for him.

Coming up behind him she sees his shabby clothes, his springing red hair hatless, and then: the unhealed cuts on the backs of his hands as he counts out a few coins of small denominations.

LUCINDA

Mr Hopkins?

Oscar spins around. He has no hat to tip, so he waves the letter he is about to post.

She sees the sore on his lip, his clerical collar gone, the pain of the last few weeks in his face, and is aware of the damage she has caused him.

Forgive me.

EXT. ROAD. LONG NOSE POINT. SYDNEY. 1869. DAY

Lucinda drives her trap along the rocky ridge of Long Nose Point. Oscar next to her, too shrouded in pain to respond either to her or to

*the light on bush and water, to the wash of clouds across the sky. His
tin trunk in the back.*

LUCINDA

I looked for you everywhere, when I read of your trouble.

OSCAR

That was kind of you.

He cannot look at her. His voice rusty.

INT. LUCINDA'S HOUSE. LONG NOSE POINT. 1869. DAY

Lucinda's maid Mrs Smith watches:

*Oscar and Lucinda at the sitting-room table. Lucinda unrolls a white
length of bandage. She takes Oscar's hand – cleaned and treated –
and bandages it:*

LUCINDA

Too tight?

*Oscar shakes head 'no'. He won't look at her. His stained clothes and
poor face make her heart break.*

One paw. Now the other.

INT. LUCINDA'S HOUSE. LONG NOSE POINT. 1869. DAY

*Mrs Smith comes into kitchen carrying the basin of water, towels over
her arm, followed by Lucinda with the rest of the first-aid things, as:*

MRS SMITH

Them cuts, they was made by praying.

LUCINDA

Not fighting?

MRS SMITH

Praying. Like this.

*And Mrs Smith is demonstrating: her fingers locked together, nails
biting into backs of hands, eyes shut, mouthing prayer.*

*Although Lucinda feels both repelled and excited by the evidence of
Oscar's agony, she also feels judged by it.*

INT. LUCINDA'S HOUSE. LONG NOSE POINT. 1869. NIGHT

Lamp on little table shows: Oscar's hands now un-bandaged. Cuts, iodine-painted, healing.

Oscar has Theophilus's little tin case open and is taking out the scrap of tissue, unfolding it, to look at his caul. The row of soldering irons in case. Bible open on table. A little line of coins piled in their denominations.

A knock on door. Oscar doesn't move.

> LUCINDA
> (*off screen*)

Mr Hopkins?

Oscar doesn't answer.

INT. LUCINDA'S HOUSE. LONG NOSE POINT. 1869. NIGHT

Lucinda listens at Oscar's door. Silence. A line of light under door.

She picks up cat and puts her face into fur, for consolation, as she walks away from Oscar's room.

EXT. FORESHORE. LONG NOSE POINT. 1869. DAY

Little strip of sand and rock at the foot of the rise up to Lucinda's house, unseen from here. Lucinda's wrap and towel on rock.

Lucinda breaststrokes in harbour.

Oscar parts grasses and undergrowth with a long stick as he walks by the harbour. He is sweating, burrs on his clothes. This walk – everything he does – is more penance than pleasure. The sky too bright, the harbour too blue, the birds too raucous.

EXT. HARBOUR ROCKS. LONG NOSE POINT. 1869. DAY

Lucinda wading out of water, on to sandy strip of foreshore.

Oscar, looking down, embarrassed to see her. He quickly clambers away, making:

Lucinda look up at him, as she puts her wrap on over her neck-to-knee bathing clothes.

EXT. BEACH TRACK. LONG NOSE POINT. DAY

Lucinda exasperated to see Oscar once again avoiding her.

> LUCINDA
> (*calls*)

Mr Hopkins?

Oscar cornered. Waits, but won't look at her as:

Lucinda climbs rocks to where he stands.

May I ask you something?

> OSCAR

I have been searching for work as a clerk. I shall not trouble you for much longer.

> LUCINDA

No, no, what I wanted to ask is, why do you avoid me?

Oscar surprised, by her heartfelt tone, into finally looking at her.

I know you have been through awful pain, and I am sorry for it. But now you hide in your room, I never see you, and when I do you will not look at me nor barely speak to me.

> OSCAR

I cannot gamble again.

> LUCINDA

I have not asked you to gamble.

> OSCAR

I am in constant fear every moment of the day that something we say or do will start it all over again.

Lucinda relieved: at last an explanation.

> LUCINDA

I admit, yes, in that case we do not have a good history.

She smiles at him. He cannot return it.

> OSCAR

I am weak. It is like opium to me. For years I gambled and took only what I needed and gave the rest to the poor. I gambled for a purpose. There was no sin in what I did. But then, when I had all my needs paid for, I still could not stop. Even when I promised God.

> LUCINDA

We shall make a pact.

> OSCAR

We shall?

> LUCINDA

To never gamble again. I promise I shall never invite you to a game of cards or any other form of gambling.

Lucinda holds out her hand to shake.

We shall keep it and be friends.

Oscar and Lucinda shake hands.

INT. LUCINDA'S HOUSE. LONG NOSE POINT. 1869. DAY

Mrs Smith hurries down stairs, with suitcase and carpet bag, as Lucinda comes from back of house into front hall, still in her damp wrap over bathing clothes, hair loose and damp.

> MRS SMITH

I am leaving. I cannot stay.

> LUCINDA

What do you mean?

> MRS SMITH

The 'gentleman' so called. I have been told who he is.

> LUCINDA

Your friends at church have been talking to you.

> MRS SMITH

I cannot stay.

> LUCINDA

Do not stay, then.

MRS SMITH

It will give me a bad name. People would think I was part of it.

LUCINDA

Part of what?

But Mrs Smith is out the front door. Lucinda, furious, kicks it shut behind her.

INT. LUCINDA'S HOUSE. LONG NOSE POINT. 1869. DAY

Lucinda at one end of tiled hall, with bucket, brush and cloth.

Oscar at the other end, with bucket, brush and cloth.

Both on hands and knees, scrubbing and wiping vigorously. This has become a competition.

Lucinda reaches the mid-point just before Oscar.

Oscar finishes. Looks up.

OSCAR

Pipped at the post.

Lucinda laughs. The cat walks across the wet floor.

INT. LUCINDA'S HOUSE. LONG NOSE POINT. 1869. NIGHT

Night. The whole house cleaned. A few little Christmas decorations.

INT. KITCHEN. LUCINDA'S HOUSE. LONG NOSE POINT. 1869.
NIGHT

*The kitchen scrubbed and cleaned. Stove blacked, fire-place red-leaded.
Oscar and Lucinda both with sleeves rolled up. Lucinda's shoes
kicked off, Oscar conscious of her stockinged feet. Her hair in cloudy
tendrils half out of its clips, Oscar's a wild blaze of peaks. A sherry
decanter, engraved with an emu, between them on the kitchen table,
a plate of shortbread, each with a glass of sherry.*

LUCINDA

I wish . . . I had ten sisters.

Oscar hoots:

OSCAR

Ten!

LUCINDA

Then maybe I could let people be simple 'good chaps', as
my father could. I am too critical.

OSCAR

Is this your confession?

They smile at this echo of the ship.

LUCINDA

And you?

OSCAR

I wish . . . I could walk on the path between the high downs
and the sea, where my father lives.

A pause between them, at this tone of tender longing.

I do not 'fit'. I know that.

LUCINDA

You do not give a hoot what people think of you.

OSCAR

My friend from Home, Wardley-Fish, thought it was of no matter.

Oscar fidgets, jiggles his foot. Lucinda looks at him as though she has never seen him before.

LUCINDA

He is right, your friend.

Oscar's smile comes and goes in the face of this intimacy.

INT. KITCHEN. LUCINDA'S HOUSE. LONG NOSE POINT. 1869. NIGHT

Oscar alone. He looks down to Lucinda's shoes on the floor, lying where she kicked them off. He bends down and picks them up. They speak to him of Lucinda. They hold the shape of her feet and feel too intimate. Embarrassed, he puts them back, as they were.

As Oscar straightens, he sees the painfully familiar fat letter addressed to The Reverend Dennis Hasset, propped up on the kitchen mantelpiece. As he picks up the letter, looking at the name:

(*voice-over*)

The idea that Lucinda loved Dennis Hasset had taken hold and would not easily be knocked loose.

INT. GLASSWORKS. SYDNEY. 1869. DAY

Inside the glory-hole: the molten metal, white-hot.

The gatherer draws it out: a red-hot orb on end of long rod.

Oscar, beside foreman Arthur Phelps, is centre of a group of glassworkers gathered around the glory-hole. Lucinda on edge of group, miffed to see Oscar being treated as Master.

The rod passes from man to man, glory-hole to glory-hole – acquiring more metal, being blown a little, swung, passed on.

ARTHUR

It is a great pleasure, sir, to see our missus take up with such a gentleman as you. When we have the window-making in full-tilt, just come along and we will be pleased to explain it to you.

OSCAR

Thank you, Arthur, I will.

Oscar watches as Arthur sits on his wooden throne, takes the long rod and transforms the metal into a glass tankard. He takes a snake of red elastic glass and, with a flourish, forms a handle.

Lucinda's little spurt of jealous anger at the way Oscar is being treated dies down when she sees that Oscar is astonished, absorbed by the beautiful miracle of transformation.

INT. GLASSWORKS. SYDNEY. 1869. DAY

Lucinda's hand lifting a cloth, like a magician, to reveal:

A model of a glass building, standing on a table in Lucinda's office.

Lucinda shy for a second, seeing her secret project through someone else's eyes. It is suddenly ordinary: a dumpy little structure.

She looks up at Oscar.

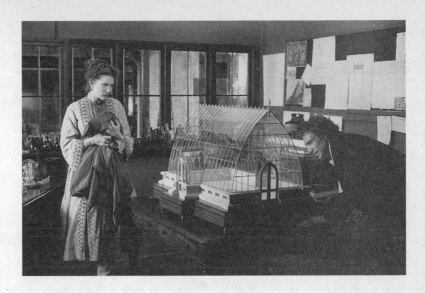

But Oscar is entranced.

LUCINDA
(*dry*)
You may approach. It is not sacred. It is only a prototype.

Oscar crouches to look into the little building. Lucinda sees that his passion equals hers. Oscar stands and walks around the glass structure.

OSCAR
It is like a kennel, for God's angels.

Lucinda laughs.

I am bowled over.

He wraps his arms around himself. On the other side of the glass building, Lucinda mirrors his action.

I feel extraordinarily happy.

They stare at each other across the glass. The power of its magic for them.

Lucinda feels the space between them a living thing.

I have an idea. Are you curious?

> LUCINDA

Of course I am curious.

As they leave the office, we briefly stay on the glass model:

> NARRATOR
> (*voice-over*)

Oscar's idea was born out of Christianity: that if you sacrifice yourself you will attain the object of your desires.

INT. ORIENTAL HOTEL. SYDNEY. 1869. NIGHT

In the cavernous luxury of a pillared half-empty dining-room, Oscar and Lucinda are at a table:

> NARRATOR
> (*voice-over*)

The odds were surely stacked against him. Had it been a horse, rather than a woman's heart, he would never have bet on it, not even for a place.

The waiter taking away soup plates as Oscar cuts his buttered bread into nine precise pieces.

> OSCAR

How does your correspondent enjoy Boat Harbour?

Lucinda's surprise at mention of Hasset.

> LUCINDA

Well enough.

> OSCAR

Does he have a church built yet?

> LUCINDA

They still hold service above the cobbler's.

> OSCAR

Mr Hasset should have a church.

Lucinda doesn't want to talk about Hasset.

LUCINDA

What is your idea?

OSCAR

What would be his feeling, if he woke one morning, looked out of his window, and saw . . . a church.

Lucinda about to reply:

Made of glass.

The idea springs to life between them.

But the waiter is there serving fish. The business of sauce and vegetables means they can only look at each other, all feelings fused into this improbable glass vision.

As the waiter goes:

LUCINDA

A church?

OSCAR

Of glass.

LUCINDA

A glass church?

OSCAR

Yes.

A pause as it takes hold in their imaginations. Lucinda tries to shake off its seductive boldness.

LUCINDA

It is not practical.

Oscar's growing expansiveness: his arms and hands wave, his voice rises.

OSCAR

What is the practical purpose of a church? If it is only to provide shelter to Christians – and my father would take this view – then it is better to worship in cobbler's rooms. But if your church is also a celebration of God, then I

would say I am the most practical man you have spoken to all year.

Lucinda thinks about kissing and pushes it from her mind. The idea of the glass church makes them smile: it has a force of its own.

It is like the stairs at the Library. It is what they call prefabricated. You could pack it in crates and transport it by cart.

LUCINDA

Or by ship.

OSCAR

You could assemble it across the Great Dividing Range.

LUCINDA

We are mad to think of it.

OSCAR

No, no, no. Not mad.

He bangs the table, cutlery jumps. Unnoticed by them, two diners glance across curiously.

LUCINDA

Can you imagine Mr Hasset's face?

OSCAR

You will deliver it to him.

LUCINDA

I?

OSCAR

But, surely –

LUCINDA

No, I cannot leave the works.

OSCAR

You would not –

LUCINDA

It is quite impossible. They are only just recovering from my last absence.

OSCAR

Then I shall. On your behalf.

Lucinda thinks of the Leviathan *and wonders why Oscar is so jubilant.*

LUCINDA

Boat Harbour is approached by sea.

OSCAR

I shall go by land.

LUCINDA

You cannot. It is largely unmapped country.

OSCAR

You think it outside my scope?

LUCINDA

There is no shame in that.

She reaches across and pats his sleeve, would like to leave her hand there.

OSCAR

There is no truth in it either. I wager you I can do it. You
may nominate the date.

LUCINDA

This is madness.

OSCAR

I am prepared to wager you that I can have the glass church
in Boat Harbour by, say, Good Friday.

*He plucks the date out of the air. Lucinda's mood reckless, she is
hooked. The bet has a life.*

LUCINDA

And what can you bet?

OSCAR

Ten guineas.

LUCINDA

Not enough.

OSCAR

What is enough?

Tension of their silence.

What is enough?

LUCINDA

Your inheritance.

OSCAR

My father may live until he's one hundred. He is not a rich
man, anyway.

LUCINDA

It makes no difference.

OSCAR

And you will bet?

LUCINDA

The same.

                    OSCAR
The same amount?

                    LUCINDA
The same. My inheritance.

                    OSCAR
You already have it.

                    LUCINDA
Yes.

                    OSCAR
Your works?

                    LUCINDA
Yes. Everything.

                    OSCAR
You wager all that?

                    LUCINDA
Yes.

                    OSCAR
Ten weeks without even a game of penny poker and now
this.

INT. D'ABBS'S OFFICE. SYDNEY. 1869. DAY

*Amateurish drawings of a glass church, drawn by Lucinda, laid out
on Jimmy d'Abbs's desk. To d'Abbs, this is all speculation, a game,
a frivolity that will never be realized. He is humouring one of his
favourite clients and tries to hide his condescension towards her odd
companion.*

                    D'ABBS
Very pretty, this fretwork, it is quite ingenious. Ah, here is
my head clerk. Come in, Jeffris, we have a question for
you. Miss Leplastrier, Mr Hopkins.

*They murmur greetings, as Jeffris comes into the office to stand in a
formal at-ease position between a seated Oscar and Lucinda, facing
d'Abbs across his desk. Jeffris is Oscar's age, a small handsome man,*

neat, precise and self-critical, with jet-black hair, clean-shaven except for a moustache.

This is from the horse's mouth, Jeffris is quite the explorer, he has been there, up North. On the road survey, wasn't it, Jeffris? He knows all the ins and outs.

OSCAR

Would that road be of any use?

JEFFRIS

If you are carrying cargo of any sort, it would be a fool's way to go.

OSCAR

We will have cargo.

JEFFRIS

Then you must go by sea.

D'ABBS

Mr Hopkins is set on going overland.

Now Jeffris looks at Oscar and makes himself gentle, playing his cards very carefully:

JEFFRIS

Is that so?

OSCAR

I am afraid it is.

D'ABBS

He refuses the steamer.

Oscar smiles at Jeffris, who looks him up and down, sadly, as if Oscar is a beast in an abattoir.

JEFFRIS

Going by land, of course one of your main problems is the butchering habits of the blacks up North. But you must know that.

Now Jeffris has their full attention.

If you go as all the incompetents have done, smack bang

through the centre of their kingdoms, what can you expect? It is like thrusting your bare hand into a beehive, it gets them hopping mad. Ergo. You take your time, go around their boundaries, and you are left alone.

LUCINDA

Who knows these boundaries?

Like a shot:

JEFFRIS

I do.

D'ABBS

Whoa! Ease up! You are not stealing my head clerk. This is surely not serious.

But Oscar and Lucinda see Jeffris as their salvation from an impossible journey by water.

EXT. GLASSWORKS. SUSSEX STREET. SYDNEY. 1870. DAY

Jeffris, now dressed in faintly military clothes, tethers his smart little horse and trap in yard.

As he walks across gravel and puddles of yard, a glassworker passes him:

GLASSWORKER

Morning, Captain.

Jeffris nods in passing and continues on.

INT. GLASSWORKS. SYDNEY. 1870. DAY

As Jeffris walks into glassworks he sees that they are given over today to the glass church.

Jeffris walking towards Oscar, in boiler suit, surrounded by glassworkers and the foundryman and, laid out on the factory floor all around them, the various components of the glass church, all labelled. Jeffris has to conceal his distaste for this odd figure with his blazing hair, his waving hands, his lack of military discipline.

Jeffris joins Lucinda, who is watching Oscar at work, as Oscar looks up to see Jeffris:

OSCAR
(*calls*)

I am in rehearsal, Mr Jeffris. I shall need some assistance at
Boat Harbour, but it need not be skilled. I have learned to
glaze.

JEFFRIS

Excellent.

OSCAR

A lot harder than Latin verbs. No, Harry, no. That is B. It
must balance H.

*Jeffris can't help a flicker of scorn as he watches this silliness. What
he could do with all this manpower.*

LUCINDA

He is a brave man, Mr Jeffris.

JEFFRIS

He is an extraordinary chap.

LUCINDA

Far braver than you or I.

JEFFRIS

One can only respect him, ma'am.

INT. GLASSWORKS. SYDNEY. 1870. DAY

Lucinda's office now Headquarters for the expedition.

*Lists of equipment and men, bills and receipts, various maps of partly-
surveyed land, drawings of glass and cast-iron components, and
detailed architectural drawings of the glass church, pinned to various
boards around the office, show the growing scale of the expedition.*

*Ahearn studies the architectural drawings, his face a mixture of wonder
and censure:*

AHEARN

When I heard of this I could not believe it. Now I see it, I
still cannot believe it.

Lucinda tries to draw his attention to plans and maps:

LUCINDA

It is a scientific expedition. Look, here is the party, we have –

AHEARN
(over)

The Australian sun will scorch your congregation as though they are in hell itself.

He is tapping the drawings to prove his point.

LUCINDA

How kind of you to come all the way from Parramatta to tell me this.

AHEARN

Have you become so sarcastic?

LUCINDA

It is to be built beneath a tree.

AHEARN

Fiddlesticks.

LUCINDA

A shady tree, in a cool aspect.

AHEARN

It will be as hot as hell. And where will the vicar change his vestments? He is like a fish! In an aquarium! For everyone to see!

He is shouting and Lucinda shouts over him:

LUCINDA

Please! Be calm.

AHEARN

You were given such a start in life. And now this – folly –

Lucinda pours him water from a jug:

LUCINDA

Look at it. Please. Calmly. It is beautiful. It celebrates God's name.

AHEARN
They will fry. They will curse God's name.

He drinks some water.

Have you forgotten your dear mother?

Lucinda feels this like a small blow.

You don't look well, girlie.

And she doesn't: skin taut, shadows under eyes, a feverish quality.

EXT./INT. ANGLICAN CHURCH. DEVON. 1870. DAY

Betty Stratton runs – distressed, awkward – out of church door.

As she leaves the church, we go inside, to see:

INT. ANGLICAN CHURCH. DEVON. 1870. DAY

Hugh Stratton hanging from rafters, above the altar.

THEOPHILUS
(*voice-over, letter*)
He has condemned himself to everlasting hellfire.

INT. HOPKINS'S COTTAGE. DEVON. 1870. DAY

THEOPHILUS
(*voice-over*)
He has cast himself out from those who can ask God's forgiveness.

Theophilus kneeling in prayer.

INT. LUCINDA'S HOUSE. LONG NOSE POINT. 1870. DAY

Oscar kneeling in prayer. Theophilus's letter open on table.

THEOPHILUS
(*voice-over*)
What brought your friend to this pass we can only conjecture.

OSCAR
Forgive me, Almighty God . . .

As he continues his silent prayer, we see a little suitcase with his few clothes in it, his Bible on top of clothes. His father's gift of the little tin case on bed.

EXT. LUCINDA'S HOUSE. LONG NOSE POINT. 1870. NIGHT

Oscar at well in yard. Jacket over pyjamas, shoes with no socks. He is drawing water. He drinks, very thirsty, from ladle.

Lucinda, in her Chinese dressing-gown, stands in kitchen doorway, looking across at Oscar.

Lucinda crossing the yard, behind Oscar.

He is startled when she comes up behind him.

They look at each other, in silence, for quite a while, as if reading each other's face.

Then they are holding each other, pressed close together.

Oscar groans. Kisses the soft warmth of Lucinda's neck. She holds him tightly, feeling his thin body fitting in to hers.

Oscar breaks away from Lucinda, then touches her again and breaks away again. The clock in the kitchen strikes two a.m.

Lucinda holds out her hands, only wanting to feel their bodies together again.

Oscar makes patting movements with his hands, in the space between them, as if to damp down their passion.

They stare at each other, the physical distance between them painful.

Oscar silently asks God not to allow him to lead Lucinda into sin. She loves Hasset. Then why go through this danger, this crippling fear? So she will love him.

Oscar wills himself to turn and walks back across the yard, leaving Lucinda at the well, watching him go.

INT. LUCINDA'S OFFICE. GLASSWORKS. SYDNEY. 1879. DAY

Through a wall of glass panels we see:

The activity around a huge cart, partly loaded with crates holding the glass church. Glassworkers help men from the expedition party load the remaining crates.

Jeffris walking across the warehouse towards Lucinda's office.

Oscar and Lucinda watching through the glass panels of her office. Both sick at heart with this leave-taking.

Jeffris appears in the doorway of Lucinda's office:

LUCINDA
Mr Jeffris?

Jeffris joins them in the office, at the wall of glass overlooking the activity of the warehouse. Lucinda is holding out an envelope to him:

I am offering you a bonus. Mr Hopkins will give this to you when he has been safely delivered.

OSCAR
Please, no.

Lucinda sees Jeffris scorns her for this. And that Oscar is humiliated by her patronizing bonus.

As she gives Oscar the envelope, she could weep.

Jeffris steps closer to the glass panels and watches the satisfying sight of the carts being loaded ready for the expedition: his ambition realized.

As Lucinda's hand finds Oscar's and tightly holds it:

So.

LUCINDA

So?

Jeffris turns back to them, impatient to leave:

JEFFRIS

Mr Hopkins?

He waits for a second:

If you please.

OSCAR

Oh, dear.

LUCINDA

Surely he can wait?

JEFFRIS

Mr Hopkins must lead the expedition.

Oscar squeezes Lucinda's hand, takes a step away. But Lucinda tightens her hold, draws him awkwardly back to her. They hold each other clumsily. Lucinda kisses him.

Jeffris' impatient, barely hidden scorn as he turns his back on this display, and disappears out of the door, the sound of his feet clattering down the steps.

LUCINDA

The Lord keep you safe.

Lucinda hands Oscar a parchment scroll:

The legal document, of our wager.

Oscar pushes a folded envelope into her hand.

Goodbye.

He bends to pick up his little suitcase and his father's tin case.

Lucinda watches as he leaves the office, and listens to his footsteps on the steps.

She goes to the glass panels and watches Oscar as he crosses the warehouse. Jeffris, waiting for him, swings in beside him and the two walk together towards the huge cart.

She watches until Oscar disappears into the activity around the cart and she can no longer see him.

NARRATOR
(*voice-over*)
When Oscar talked of going overland

EXT. BRIDGE. THE ROCKS. SYDNEY. 1870. DAY

Jeffris, in red coat on his large black stallion, leads the expedition party:

NARRATOR
(*voice-over*)
he had not known there were six rivers to cross: the Macleay, the Hastings, the Clarence, the Manning, the Hunter and the Namoi.

Behind Jeffris, Oscar sits on the leading wagon, stacked with crates, pulled by a team of four horses. Oscar high up, next to the driver, his father's tin case and his suitcase balanced on his knees. Lucinda's scroll in his hand.

Oscar was sick with fear at the thing he had begun.

Behind Oscar's cart stretches a line of horses and men and carts: the full expedition party, crossing the bridge.

EXT. TUNNEL. THE ROCKS. SYDNEY. 1870. DAY

The last of the expedition, including a canvas-covered wagon, makes its way into the dark mouth of a stone tunnel arching high over a road.

INT. GLASSWORKS. SYDNEY. 1870. DAY

Through a large arched glass window, Lucinda looks down at the last of the expedition disappearing into the tunnel. She is dismayed at the size and military appearance of this thing she has created.

Then, the last horse gone, the tunnel empty, she looks down: Oscar's envelope crushed in her hand.

EXT. BARGE. SYDNEY HARBOUR. 1870. DAY

Percy Smith stands beside big stack of wooden crates. He enjoys the movement of the barge on the water.

> JEFFRIS
> *(off screen, calls)*

Smith! Smith!

Percy hurries around the crates to see:

Oscar on his back, kicking and straining, with Jeffris holding him down, trying to fit a funnel into Oscar's mouth:

Help me, man, he's having a fit!

As Percy hurries to help: to sit on Oscar's legs and hold his jaws open. Oscar's head pulling back, eyes rolling, feet kicking, groaning.

EXT. BARGE. SYDNEY HARBOUR. 1870. DAY

Oscar – now bundled into the expedition uniform – is sitting slumped against the pile of wooden crates. Dazed. Eyes shut. Traces of green liquid around his mouth. He puts up fingers to feel its stickiness.

Percy Smith and Jeffris talk above him.

> JEFFRIS

You are to supervise him at all times. You are not to let him out of your sight. When you hold your roger, you will have your eye on him. When you wipe your arsehole, you will have your other hand around his ankle. When there are rivers to be forded, you will administer five fluid ounces of the laudanum.

Smith hates himself for being unable to hold Jeffris' gaze, wishes he could say no.

> PERCY
>
> And my duties as collector of animals?

> JEFFRIS
>
> All other duties are second to this one.

Jeffris hands Smith the funnel and moves up to the front of barge.

Oscar, his eyes opening to see the expanse of bright water, like metal.

The laudanum has dazed him, dulled his fear. Percy Smith's legs in front of him, his hand holding the funnel. The motion of the barge through the water. The fainter sound of horses and men from other barges. The blinding light on the water. Oscar closes his eyes.

EXT. MANGROVE SWAMPS. NSW. 1870. LATE AFTERNOON

Amongst the dark twisted trunks of mangrove trees:

A cart, carrying crates of glass, is stuck in the mud of the mangrove swamp.

Men behind the cart, pushing. The cart's driver, off the cart, pulling his horse's bridle, urging him out of the mud. Shouts of the men as they heave and push. The horse's whinnying. Jeffris barking orders.

All this activity watched by Percy, under a little canvas awning, on the seat of his wagon. He turns to check Oscar, on the seat beside him:

Oscar coming out of his laudanum daze.

> PERCY
>
> Does your throat still pain you?

> OSCAR
>
> It is not so bad.

> PERCY
>
> If I coat the funnel with wax, when you have your fits –

> OSCAR
>
> I had no fit.

PERCY

I found you in one.

Jeffris, marching down the waiting expedition, barely pauses beside Oscar. He doesn't bother to conceal his scornful anger:

JEFFRIS

This damn church of yours, sir, is costing us time.

As Jeffris moves on:

OSCAR

He forced his 'medicine' upon me. I had no fit.

PERCY

He fears your phobia, that you will throw yourself into the water.

OSCAR

He fears he will lose his bonus. But he will not lose me. I will be here until the end. I have much to live for.

INT. LUCINDA'S HOUSE. LONG NOSE POINT. 1870. NIGHT

NARRATOR
(*voice-over*)

That she did not open Oscar's letter was not forgetfulness. She did not wish to weep. They would carry him safely, and they would bring him back.

Lucinda propped up in bed, her cat draped across her lap, Oscar's envelope lies on the cat's fur, gently rising and falling.

She takes Oscar's envelope and for a brief moment stares at the envelope, then quickly tears it open, and reads:

OSCAR
(*voice-over*)

I dare not hope, and yet I must, that through this deed, I gain your trust.

LUCINDA

You had my trust!

She wills herself not to cry.

You fool. My darling.

She lifts Oscar's letter, covering her face with it.

Lucinda did not know she would have to wait six weeks
before the next steamer left for Boat Harbour.

EXT. STEEP TRACK. RAWSON FALLS. NSW. 1870. DAY

Giant palms and ferns in deep bush. Greenish light.

*Up a steep incline, rocks crash down past Oscar and Percy in their
wagon. Specimen cages of animals: cockatoos, a wallaby, secured in
back of wagon.*

*Oscar – sunburnt, insect-bitten – jolts on the seat beside Percy. Sounds
of men calling, horses, shouted commands, from ahead of them in
the bush.*

*Percy sees Jeffris riding towards them down the line of the toiling
expedition.*

*Jeffris – as spruce as always, even in these circumstances – wheels his
horse to turn and ride beside them:*

JEFFRIS
How goes life in the Ladies Compartment?

Oscar ignores him. Jeffris insists:

What do you say to this, the countryside?

Oscar only briefly glances at Jeffris, his voice drugged by laudanum:

OSCAR
If it were my country, sir, I would be feared to see you
coming.

*Jeffris laughs: harsh, impatient, and puts his horse into a trot and we
go with him along the line of men, horses, cargo, up the incline.
Amongst the expedition, we briefly see: the young carpenter, hands
tied behind him, his shirt bloody on his back from being lashed. We see:
two Aboriginal men from the Narcoo tribe, who have joined the*

*expedition. We see: Jeffris reaching out with his stick to come down
thwack! on the hand of a man who is fumbling a rope.*

NARRATOR
(*voice-over*)
In a laudanum daze, Oscar dreamed he was in his father's
aquarium, the water soothing to his burnt skin. He dreamed
of his mother's buttons, covered over with floating fronds of
seaweed.

*Oscar, on the wagon next to Percy, takes out little flask, half-full of
laudanum, sips from it, then puts it back into his pocket.*

EXT. CAMP. MOUNT DAWSON. NSW. 1870. NIGHT

*Horses tethered near the dark perimeter of bush around the expedition's
camp.*

*Tents shadowy in darkness, a few with lamplight shining through
canvas. Only one camp-fire burning, with a few men around it,
drinking. Two Scots singing:*

TWO SCOTS
(*sing*)
I wae tell ye a tale o'angel named Beggs,
Came down tae earth, silk purse tween ha legs.

*In the dense bush around the camp a few flame-lights begin to appear,
flickering intermittently through the bush, coming closer.*

*The horses restive, as two unarmed Kumbaingiri elders step out of the
bush, holding firesticks.*

*One of the men around the camp-fire looks over at the horses, and
sees the Kumbaingiri men. He stands, shouting. The other men around
the camp-fire shout:*

MEN
(*various, call*)
Blacks! Niggers! Hoy! Captain!

*The two Narcoo men run towards the Kumbaingiri, as men come out
of tents, some drunk, some half-asleep. Oscar and Percy amongst
them, raised by the alarm.*

The Kumbaingiri and Narcoo men talking together:

> KUMBAINGIRI
> (*various*)
>
> Who are these strangers? What are they doing in our
> country? Why have you brought them here? We have come to
> talk with them.

> NARCOO MEN
>
> They carry magic boxes to Bellingen. We are showing them
> the way. They will not harm you.

*Jeffris has come out of his tent. He walks towards the Narcoo and
Kumbaingiri men.*

*He sees more of the Kumbaingiri men coming out of the bush, holding
firesticks.*

He raises his pistol and shoots.

A Kumbaingiri boy of about fourteen drops to the ground.

On Oscar, as he starts to run towards the blacks, shouting:

> OSCAR
>
> No, Jeffris! Talk to them! Stop! In God's name! Do not
> shoot!

*Men running everywhere, arming themselves with axes and pistols.
Shooting. Chaos. Oscar runs on, past Jeffris. Percy sprinting after
him.*

> JEFFRIS
>
> Tie that fool up!

Percy tackles Oscar to the ground.

EXT. TAVERN YARD. URUNGA. NSW. 1870. DAY

*A tavern surrounded by a little settlement of grey, neglected tents.
Sound of men's voices and laughter from tavern.*

The wagons empty. Horses tethered. Dogs hang about.

Percy sits on wagon seat, honing his axe.

Oscar, now dressed in his black clerical suit and white collarless shirt, walks from back of wagon to front. His wrists are raw from rope-burns, the left wrist wears a brown-stained bandage.

OSCAR

Come, Smith.

PERCY

Oh, God, man. Surely you are not going to drink with them?

OSCAR

I have already travelled with them.

Small black flies everywhere. Percy watches Oscar crossing the yard towards the tavern, flies thick across his back.

INT. TAVERN. URUNGA. NSW. 1870. DAY

Men at bar – mainly timber cutters – laughing and looking across at:

Oscar, a curiosity in his black suit, his flaming hair, his fine, burnt face. He glares out at the bar from a table against the wall.

Jeffris, centre of group at bar, buying drinks.

JEFFRIS

He is a padre. Come to bring God to Bellingen.

The men's natural belligerence towards the church heats up their antagonism to this oddity on their territory.

Jeffris gives champagne to blacksmith:

Take this over. And keep your eye on him. He's not to leave.

At this moment, Oscar is his father's son. He would burn the tavern down, bring retribution to the wicked.

A torn curtain, in wall at right-angle to him, reveals a glimpse of a naked white man and Aboriginal woman on a bed. Men come and go through the curtain.

The blacksmith and the expedition's young carpenter sit with Oscar at his table. He sips champagne.

As man bumps up to the table, makes a flourishing bow, gestures to the curtain:

MAN

Step through, dip your wee white toe in the holy well.

As publican's wife delivers two ales to Oscar:

PUBLICAN'S WIFE

With the compliments of Sir Roger Rogerer and Lord
Pupslaughter.

*Laughter and whistles from bar. The frightened carpenter spills his
drink on table.*

Oscar glances down: the boy's lips moving in prayer.

*Jeffris, nervous of a tavern brawl in this overheated atmosphere, puts
his hand on his sword.*

As Oscar stands, to a cheer, then dying noise.

Only the sound of a woman crying quietly on other side of the curtain.

Silence. Oscar wonders: what would God have me do?

He raises his hand.

He watches, as everyone watches, his wrist emerging from frayed sleeve.

Oscar's voice clear in bar:

OSCAR

How thin my wrist is. This wrist God made for me.

No one speaks or moves.

How could I smite you?

Oscar is not afraid. He feels great clarity.

*He watches his hand. With his other hand he pats his pockets for
laudanum flask, draws it out: empty.*

But he has found something else in his pocket.

I will play you poker and I will win. This money will be your
gift to God's work in Boat Harbour.

He draws out Lucinda's bonus envelope: holds it up:

JEFFRIS
(*shouts*)

No!

OSCAR

I have a pot of one hundred pounds.

JEFFRIS
(*shouts, over*)

I forbid it!

Jeffris leaves the bar. General noise now.

OSCAR
(*above noise*)

I would shoot you dead and go to hell for it.

Oscar pushes table out of way.

You murderer.

*No one tries to stop Jeffris, who moves towards Oscar through crowd
of men, his sword drawn.*

Oscar stands, back straight, voice clear, as Jeffris comes closer:

The Lord is my shepherd. I shall not want. Thou preparest a table for me in the presence of mine enemies –

Jeffris grabs Oscar's arm above the elbow and yanks him so hard he cries out with pain, knocking table aside.

JEFFRIS

Out!

OSCAR
(*over*)

I warn you –

JEFFRIS
(*shrieks, over*)

Out, now!

Jeffris is dragging Oscar from the tavern, through the laughing, cheering, clapping, whistling men.

Oscar's outrage, pain, impotence. The envelope held high, away from Jeffris, in his hand.

EXT. TAVERN URUNGA. NSW. 1870. DAY

Percy sits on wagon seat – his tomahawk and honing stone in hands – watches as:

Jeffris, his sword raised, kicking Oscar as he half-crawls, half-staggers across the yard.

Oscar takes refuge beneath the wagon.

Jeffris kicks under wagon with his boot. His sword pokes between spokes of wheel.

Oscar out the other side, trying to clamber up steps to the seat beside Percy:

OSCAR

God help me.

Jeffris suddenly behind Oscar, grabs his shoulder, pulling him back.

Percy raises his tomahawk and brings it down on Jeffris' upper arm.

He feels great pleasure as the tomahawk cuts into bone.

Jeffris stumbles back from wagon, blood spurting through bright red cloth of coat.

Oscar lifts the axe: its glinting blade.

He stands with feet astride, on the step, the axe held incorrectly, hands too close together.

Oscar screams as:

He brings the axe down on to Jeffris' gleaming, brilliantined head.

Oscar's hands spring away from axe handle, quivering and clapping with tension and fear.

Jeffris kneels, slips forward, the axe in his skull.

Percy checks: the yard empty of men.

He pulls blanket from seat and jumps down and wraps it around Oscar and brings him down to ground and, without thinking, he swaddles him like a baby, stilling Oscar's shaking body with force.

EXT. BELLINGER RIVER. NSW. 1870. DAY

Inside tent, Oscar cocooned in checked blanket, in sticky heat. He opens his eyes. He sees morning light through the familiar stained canvas. His little suitcase and his father's tin case beside him. He hears the sound of someone whistling and hammering.

EXT. BELLINGER RIVER. NSW. 1870. DAY

Outside the tent: Oscar has crawled out, dazed, squinting. He stands. Turns to the sound of whistling, hammering.

He sees the cool blue stretch of the Bellinger River: a wide still sheet of water with a rough little wharf built out over it. Someone hammering and whistling below wharf.

Oscar on wharf, still dazed, barely seeing anything around himself, looks down to:

Percy on barge below wharf, holding hammer, grinning up at Oscar.

OSCAR

Did I not murder a man?

PERCY

We did.

OSCAR

Where is our party?

PERCY

They're off. Gone south. In pursuit of Mr Jeffris.

Oscar can't understand Percy's gentle high spirits.

He went off with their pay, so they believe, so they have chased after him.

OSCAR
(*groans*)

Oh, Lord.

Percy up on to wharf to help swaying Oscar.

PERCY

Whoa, there. Whoa, Neddy.

As Percy guides Oscar back to solid ground of river bank:

There, there, you must not fear.

OSCAR

I have killed a man.

PERCY

It is a bad man we have killed. Your maker will forgive you. In truth, I have felt more sorrow to have slain a beast.

But Oscar knows he is damned. Percy sits him on log next to ashes of fire.

They were nice enough to leave us tea and sugar and a billy. For the rest, they were in too much of a hurry.

Oscar stands.

OSCAR

My church.

He looks around wildly, dazed. Percy can't help laughing.

Look around you.

Now Oscar focuses, looking around more carefully: spread around them are the crates of glass, the hessian-wrapped iron pieces, the bags of nuts and bolts, the containers of putty and oil, all with little labels fluttering in the wind.

EXT. STEAMER. NSW COAST. 1870. DAY

Across an expanse of ocean, Lucinda's little steamer makes its way up the coast.

INT. LUCINDA'S CABIN. STEAMER. 1870. DAY

Lucinda's hands flying over cards laid out for patience. Her tiny cabin, the movement of the steamer, the sound of the engine. For a moment she looks up, as if listening.

EXT. TREVIS FARM. BELLINGER RIVER. NSW. 1870. DAY

Miriam – the governess – no longer in mourning, walks up and down verandah to quieten the crying baby over her shoulder. Her beautiful long black hair is freshly washed and spread to dry on towel over her shoulders.

Mrs Trevis, dressed for town, comes out on to verandah. Her little girl and boy run down steps across to horse and trap.

MRS TREVIS
I'll take bubba, Miriam.

Miriam hands bubba to Mrs Trevis, who looks critically at Miriam's rose dress.

Tt-tt-tt. It's tempting fate to have thrown away your widow's weeds.

MIRIAM
Why? I have no one left to mourn for. My father, my mother, my husband. They're all gone.

MRS TREVIS
If you had nabbed young Reverend Hasset –

MIRIAM

I did not attempt to 'nab' him, poor man, although he's been properly 'nabbed' now.

Mrs Trevis going down steps, holding crying bubba, as:

MRS TREVIS

Jealousy killed the cat.

MIRIAM
(*calls*)

Curiosity.

MRS TREVIS
(*calls over*)

Don't forget to do the butter.

MIRIAM
(*to herself*)

Not jealousy.

EXT. TREVIS FARM. BELLINGER RIVER. NSW. 1870. DAY

Miriam – head bent forward, shaking her hair to dry it – swings her head back up, her hair flying up to settle in soft black cloak over her shoulders.

She looks out, over the paddocks, down to the sweep of river below the house.

Into the view comes: a glass church, floating up river.

Miriam's astonishment as she stands on the top step of the verandah and stares down at this apparition:

The little steep-roofed church with its decorative black cast-iron skeleton, its tall, thin, arched panes of glass, a cross at the tip of the gable of the pitched roof. Three men, with poles, steer its course up river, moving around the perimeter of the barge which holds the church.

EXT. BELLINGER RIVER. NSW. 1870. MIRIAM'S POV

As the church slews in the river, the sun strikes it at another angle: it goes from opaque to transparent and Miriam sees:

A black-suited figure seated on chair in the centre of the church.

EXT. TREVIS FARM. BELLINGER RIVER. NSW. 1870. DAY

Practical concerns swamp Miriam's sense of wonder.

EXT. RIVER BANK. BELLINGER RIVER. NSW. 1870. DAY

Miriam cantering – her pony refuses to walk – down the rutted hill towards the river.

EXT. PATH. BELLINGER RIVER. NSW. 1870. DAY

Miriam, now almost in a gallop, on the cattle path above the river.

She comes up beside the glass church and the men poling the barge.

Self-conscious, embarrassed, she cannot slow her pony down to a walk.

EXT./INT. CHURCH. BELLINGER RIVER. NSW. 1870. DAY

Percy Smith and two men as they pole away stray cedar logs coming down river, keeping the church on course. The men's voices as they call to each other, navigating the currents.

We see a few panes of glass are cracked, splintered. Oscar, seen through glass, on his chair, in his black suit.

Oscar, his small suitcase beside bentwood chair, sits in the very centre of the church.

Water surrounds him, flowing past the glass walls which reflect and hold sunlight and shadows and waterlight.

Shadows pass across Oscar's face from trees on steep riverbank. He takes the caul out of its tissue paper and holds it as he prays:

OSCAR
Oh, Lord, all Thy glory surrounds me, but I am afraid.

Deep green banks covered in thick bush down to the river's edge: reflected in the water.

The river rippling out, long streamers of light, from the wash of the barge.

Oscar sweating, sunburnt, in the heat of the glass church.

He looks up to the three cracked – but still in place – glass panes in the roof.

Percy Smith drives his pole hard into the river mud.

The platform beneath Oscar's feet twists.

Another pane cracks and splinters. This time glass falls to the wooden floor.

Oh Lord, I thank Thee for granting me this day.

For answer, three more panes crack, but hold.

Oscar takes off his jacket and lifts it on to his head, draping it so it hangs like a hood over the back of his head, cloaking him.

EXT. ROCKY RIDGE. BELLINGER RIVER. NSW. 1870. DAY

A small group – men, women, and children – of the Kumbaingiri tribe on high rocky ridge above river.

They are exclaiming, talking to each other, as they watch:

The glass church floating up the deep green of the river. Oscar, from this distance, looks like a nun sitting in the church.

EXT. WHARF. BOAT HARBOUR. NSW. 1870. DAY

The wharf crowded with people. At the head of the crowd is Dennis Hasset, in correct clerical black, with the Government Inspector and his clerk. The crowd noisy, expectant, ready to be amazed, in need of entertainment.

A distant view of the church, now almost opaque.

The crowd's astonishment: its excited conjectures, argument, as:

NARRATOR
(*voice-over*)
Dennis Hasset thought many things at once. That it was a miracle, a broken thing, a tragedy, a dream, a . . .

HASSET
(*low*)

... Lucinda! ...

INT. GLASS CHURCH. WHARF. BOAT HARBOUR. NSW. 1870. DAY

*Percy helps Oscar on with his jacket. Hands him his little suitcase,
and his father's tin case:*

OSCAR

Are we there, Percy?

PERCY

Yes. They are all waiting.

Sound of crowd outside. The glass almost opaque.

EXT. WHARF. BOAT HARBOUR. NSW. 1870. DAY

Hasset watches, wishes this weren't happening.

Miriam, coming through the crowd, in her aqua riding-habit.

*The crowd's noise dies to just a murmur, then almost to silence, as
Oscar is led by Percy Smith out of the door and is seen clearly for
the first time:*

*This strange, oddly impressive, figure, carrying his little case, in his
old black suit, his burnt skin, his flaming hair, his sense of purpose
which could be laughable but isn't.*

Percy Smith walks with Oscar up the wharf steps:

PERCY
(*quiet*)

There you are, Mr Hopkins. Safe and dry.

OSCAR

Thank you, Percy. I will go alone, now.

Oscar sees Dennis Hasset at head of crowd.

The Government Inspector engages Percy in talk about moorings.

Oscar making his way towards Hasset.

He holds a fixed gaze on the uncomfortable Hasset.

Sir.

Oscar holds out a hand. The two men shake hands.

The Reverend Mr Hasset?

Oscar will not release Hasset's eyes, not for a second. Hasset feels sick.

HASSET

Yes.

Oscar's voice, loud and clear in this public presentation, for a moment overcomes the agony of the journey, in the knowledge that he has won his wager with Lucinda, that he is almost there.

OSCAR

Then I have the pleasure sir . . . to present this splendid church to you. It is a gift to the Christians of Boat Harbour – all these people – from the most wonderful woman in New South Wales. How you can stand there when Miss Leplastrier pines in Sydney . . . is quite . . . beyond my . . .

Oscar shuddering now, his face contorted.

Hasset puts a hand on his shoulder. Oscar sways with pain and exhaustion.

Hasset, tense with anxiety, looks around for help. Most of the crowd are examining the church.

With relief, he sees Miriam:

HASSET

Mrs Chadwick?

Miriam joins them:

Would you help us?

From Percy's point of view: Oscar going off, being led between Hasset and Miriam. He turns back to mooring business with Inspector, clerk and his two helpers.

EXT. POST OFFICE. BOAT HARBOUR. NSW. 1870. DAY

Oscar stands in shade, supported by Post Office wall, the strain too much for his body and spirit to bear.

A few steps away Hasset and Miriam confer.

> HASSET

I must hurry home before my wife hears all this puffed up by gossips. Would you be the Good Samaritan? Here is a crown. Buy him bandages and whatever he needs. The key to the meeting room. Lock the door to keep out busybodies. Look after him, the poor beggar. Can you manage? Will Mrs Trevis permit you?

> MIRIAM

Dear Dennis, hurry home to Mary. Leave this wounded soul to me.

Going away from us: Miriam holds Oscar's arm, his little suitcase in her other hand. She lets him lean on her as they walk very slowly down beside the Post Office.

INT. ANGLICAN ROOMS. BOAT HARBOUR. NSW. 1870. DAY

An altar set up, cross on wall behind it, rows of bentwood chairs, make an approximation of a church.

In little store-room off main meeting room:

Oscar lies on rug on floor, a folded cloth under his head.

Miriam has set up a little arsenal of ointments, lotions and bandages, a bowl of water, cloths. Her hat perched on cabinet.

She stands above Oscar, looking down at him, her eyes full of pity and purpose.

Oscar's hands twitch on rug, his body twitching and shuddering. His fine, poor, burnt skin, his worn clerical clothes.

> MIRIAM

You poor, poor man. What trials have you been through?

Miriam kneels behind him.

There-there. There-there.

She tenderly lifts him up in her arms and peels off his clerical coat.

He is shuddering, eyes open, staring up at her.

Then eyes shut. His body obedient, grateful for her tender touch.

She leans him against her thighs and undoes his shirt and gently, tenderly takes it off.

His neck, hands and face burnt. His arms and chest a tender white, bruised and scratched.

She lies him back down.

She touches his hair, gently brushing it back and up from his forehead.

His face turning one way then the other.

Oscar moaning. Miriam making small noises of comfort.

Miriam at his feet, undoing his boots and dropping them, first one then the other – ruined things – behind her on the floor: thud thud.

OSCAR

Dear God.

She peels off his socks. His fine white bony feet.

She kneels back and looks at him. A long shudder goes through his body.

She puts her hands on his ankles, holding them. Her hands slide up his legs.

Oscar groans. Not only a groan of pain now, but also of sexual arousal.

Miriam stands and – under her skirt – takes off her bloomers.

She hitches her skirts up and gently, carefully, sits astride Oscar.

Miriam looks down at her conquest: she will not lose this one.

Under her skirts, she undoes Oscar's trousers and as she puts her hand on his penis he gives a long giant groan of sexual recognition and desire.

133

Miriam guides him into her and she starts moving on top of him.

EXT. GOVERNMENT PADDOCK. BOAT HARBOUR. NSW. 1870. LATE
AFTERNOON

From a distance we watch:

*Miriam and Oscar crossing the paddock where horses and ponies are
tethered.*

NARRATOR
(*voice-over*)
Although his whole heart cried out for Lucinda, Oscar
believed that he would have to marry this woman he had
compromised. It did not occur to him that she had
compromised him. That he had been 'nabbed'.

*Oscar, holding open the gate of the government paddock, half bows as
Miriam walks her pony through the gate, holding a tight rein on the
pony's mouth.*

Oscar closes the gate and stands, at a loss, looking around him.

He sees a stick on the ground. Idly, he picks it up.

*The last light of afternoon, soft across the paddock, casts long
shadows. The glistening river beyond the paddock: a line of water.
He starts to walk across the paddock towards the river, trailing the
stick behind him, leaving a wavering line in the dust.*

EXT./INT. WHARF/GLASS CHURCH. BELLINGER RIVER. NSW.
1870. DAY

High tide. Mooring ropes creaking, stretched.

Oscar's boots on planks of little wharf.

Little girl runs past with dog on riverbank, glancing at:

Oscar going down wharf steps towards moored church.

*Oscar walks into church, full of darkening waterlight, closing cedar
door behind him.*

Walks across splintered glass and dead insects.

He sits on the bentwood chair. The faint creaking movement of the barges. He bows his head to pray for forgiveness:

OSCAR

Forgive me, Almighty God, for the murder of the blacks.
Forgive me for the death of Mr Stratton. Forgive me for
the murder of Mr Jeffris. Forgive me, Almighty God, for the
seduction of Mrs Chadwick. Forgive me for my pride,
forgive me for my ignorance. Forgive me for betraying
Lucinda.

His hands locked together, nails digging into backs of hands, as he sways on chair. But he feels himself polluted almost beyond redemption.

And my father. Will we never again stand together?

From the riverbank – through splintered glass and darkening light – Oscar is only a dim shape in church. The riverbank deserted. Wind blows leaves of trees and casts a long rippling pattern on the evening water

EXT. WHARF. BOAT HARBOUR. NSW. A FEW HOURS LATER. 1870.
DUSK

Oscar asleep: head bowed on chest, his breathing rough and deep, in his exhausted sleep.

The lighter further away from the riverbank – of the two lighters that make up the barge – has been shipping water. Now, with a final wash of water:

The platform drops on one side. Water rushes over the platform, rising into the church.

Chair tilts. Oscar hits the floor. Wakes.

Slides and slips down to the lower side, further from the door.

He scrambles up the slope towards the door, but when Oscar reaches the door he finds that the twisting platform has jammed it shut. Oscar pulls and kicks at the jammed door.

Not quite dark. Flying foxes fill the sky above the river. The tilting platform becomes a ramp and the glass church slides easily into the accepting river.

Oscar shakes his head, panicking in the face of eternity.

Briefly, Lucinda puts out her hand to an unseen Oscar at the well.

The water rises. The doorknob becomes the ceiling of his world.

Briefly, Theophilus smiles at Oscar, looking at him through the glass of his aquarium.

As the water rises to Oscar's mouth, he screams. The water fills the church. Oscar's body, like a sea-creature, floats down through the water, turning and turning, in a giant aquarium.

EXT. GRAVEYARD. OUTSIDE BELLINGEN. NSW. 1870. DAY

A cleared paddock on a hill: twenty or so graves dotted, arbitrarily it seems, here and there. All around, the profound silence of the vast country spreading out to the horizon.

A hot wind blows across the tiny group of mourners beside a freshly dug grave, the hard red earth piled beside the grave. Two grave-diggers stand a few steps away from the mourners: Lucinda, Miriam, Percy Smith, the Government Inspector and his clerk, and Mary. Flies settle on backs, clothes and hair blow in the hot wind.

> HASSET
>
> Man that is born of woman hath but a short time to live, and is full of misery. He cometh up, and is cut down, like a flower; he fleeth as it were a shadow, and never continueth in one stay.

As Dennis Hasset officiates, Miriam can't resist slyly taking in Lucinda. She is pleased to find her no rival. The only person crying is Percy, who weeps like a baby.

Lucinda – dry-eyed – full of an odd anger, which she battles to keep in control. Her face paler and paler.

EXT. GLASS CHURCH. PADDOCK. BELLINGEN. NSW. 1870. DAY

The glass church – a twisted, water-damaged mockery of its first shining perfection – stands in a tussocky paddock.

Lucinda, in her mourning black, walks with Dennis Hasset across the paddock towards the church:

> LUCINDA
> Would you care for our church?

Hasset embarrassed:

> HASSET
> My dear . . .

> LUCINDA
> Not as it is, of course. We could surely have it made useful. Weatherboards attached, or somesuch.

Lucinda's voice flat, detached.

> HASSET
> What a gift that would be. I shall take you up on that.

Hasset pauses to survey his gift. Lucinda beside him, staring at the ruined thing. He turns to her:

Thank you.

Lucinda walks on, towards the glass church.

Hasset watches her for a second, before he turns and makes his way back across the tussocky paddock.

INT. GLASS CHURCH. PADDOCK. BELLINGEN. NSW. 1870. DAY

The glass now almost opaque from river water, many of the panes shattered. The timber floor sodden. The wooden chair lies tipped over against one wall. Almost idly, Lucinda goes to it and lifts it to set it upright. She sees, under the chair, Oscar's little tin case from his father. She bends and picks it up, almost as if she will throw it away from herself, as if disgusted. She will not cry. She knows she should not have come here.

But instead of leaving, she sits on the wooden chair where Oscar sat, his tin case on her lap.

She opens the case. Takes out the little scrap of tissue paper and unwraps it: Oscar's caul.

Her face contorts, she will not cry. But she does and, because it has been so repressed and is against her will, her crying comes out in great gasping racking sobs.

INT. HASSET'S HOUSE. BELLINGEN. NSW. 1871. EVENING

Oscar's suitcase, opened in Hasset's little makeshift study. Hasset reading the legal documents of Oscar's and Lucinda's wager:

NARRATOR
(*voice-over*)
If Miriam had known of Oscar's wager with Lucinda, she would have moved heaven and earth

Flames eating into the paper of the wager document, burning in glass pen-tray.

to claim Lucinda's fortune.

EXT. TREVIS FARM. BELLINGER RIVER. NSW. 1871. MORNING

Hot December morning and Miriam, once again in mourning black, is sitting on the top step of the verandah. Her long, freshly washed hair spread to dry on a towel over her shoulders. She is nine months pregnant:

> NARRATOR
> (*voice-over*)
> Before my great-grandmother died, she had time to see

EXT. WEATHERBOARD CHURCH. BELLINGEN. NSW. 1871. DAY

The little church, now covered in weatherboards, on its rise above the river, a few horses and traps tethered outside.

> NARRATOR
> (*voice-over*)
> that her baby had the same red hair as his father.

INT. WEATHERBOARD CHURCH. BELLINGEN. NSW. 1871. DAY

Dennis Hasset baptizes the baby: the water trickles over his newborn red hair:

> NARRATOR
> (*voice-over*)
> When Dennis Hasset told Lucinda the baby's history,

INT. GLASSWORKS. SYDNEY. 1877. DAY

> NARRATOR
> (*voice-over*)
> she had only one thought in mind.

Oscar's son, now six and with his father's red hair, swims in the harbour below Lucinda's house. He duck-dives, surfaces, plays. Calls out to Lucinda: 'Watch! Watch me, Lucinda.' Lucinda breaststrokes, watching the boy.

The water of the harbour becomes:

EXT. BELLINGER RIVER. CHURCH SITE. BELLINGEN. NSW.
PRESENT DAY

The water of the Bellinger River.

On a rise above the river:

The timber foundation-stumps of the weatherboard church.

The church now gone.

NARRATOR
(*voice-over*)

The church my great-grandfather assembled here, on this
river, shining clear, like heaven,

EXT. BELLINGER RIVER. NSW. PRESENT DAY

On river:

*A little outboard motor-boat chugs into view. A red-haired child in the
boat with his father, the Narrator.*

*We see the Narrator face-to-face for the first time. He speaks directly
to us. He could almost be Oscar:*

NARRATOR

is gone. A dream, a lie, a wager, love. This is the story
Lucinda gave to my grandfather and I give to you.

The boat disappears up the river.

*The river, as the rippling wash from the boat disappears, leaving the
reflections of the sky and deep banks in the broad sweep of still water.*

The river turns to dusk, to evening, to night, to black.

CREDITS

FOX SEARCHLIGHT PICTURES PRESENTS
IN ASSOCIATION WITH THE AUSTRALIAN FILM FINANCE CORPORATION
AND THE NEW SOUTH WALES FILM AND TELEVISION OFFICE
A DALTON FILMS PRODUCTION
A GILLIAN ARMSTRONG FILM
RALPH FIENNES
CATE BLANCHETT

OSCAR AND LUCINDA

CIARAN HINDS

TOM WILKINSON

RICHARD ROXBURGH

CLIVE RUSSELL

BILLE BROWN

JOSEPHINE BYRNES

BARNABY KAY

BARRY OTTO

LINDA BASSETT

CASTING ALISON BARRETT

KATHLEEN MACKIE

COSTUMES DESIGNED BY JANET PATTERSON

PRODUCTION DESIGNER LUCIANA ARRIGHI

DIRECTOR OF PHOTOGRAPHY GEOFFREY SIMPSON A.C.S.

FILM EDITOR NICHOLAS BEAUMAN

MUSIC BY THOMAS NEWMAN

ASSOCIATE PRODUCER MARK TURNBULL

FROM THE ORIGINAL NOVEL BY PETER CAREY

SCREENPLAY BY LAURA JONES

PRODUCED BY ROBIN DALTON & TIMOTHY WHITE

DIRECTED BY GILLIAN ARMSTRONG

NARRATOR   Geoffrey Rush

CAST IN ORDER OF APPEARANCE
YOUNG LUCINDA   Polly Cheshire
ELIZABETH LEPLASTRIER   Gillian Jones
ABEL LEPLASTRIER   Robert Menzies
YOUNG OSCAR   Adam Hayes

THEOPHILUS	Clive Russell
13-YEAR-OLD OSCAR	James Tingby
MRS WILLIAMS	Matyelok Gibbs
FANNY DRABBLE	Sonia Ritter
BETTY STRATTON	Linda Bassett
HUGH STRATTON	Tom Wilkinson
OSCAR HOPKINS	Ralph Fiennes
COLLEGE STUDENTS	Will Barton, Jonathan Markwood, Nicolas Tennant, Sam Newman, Nicholas Fordham
WARDLEY-FISH	Barnaby Kay
LUCINDA LEPLASTRIER	Cate Blanchett
MR AHEARN	Peter Whitford
MRS AHEARN	Lynette Curran
STEAMER CAPTAIN	Ron Blanchard
REVEREND DENNIS HASSET	Ciaran Hinds
FRAZER	Colin Taylor
HOTEL MAID	Michelle Doake
SOCIETY GOSSIPS	Karen Vickery, Elspeth MacTavish
JIMMY D'ABBS	Barry Otto
MISS SHADDOCK	Andrea Moor
MISS MALCOLM	Leverne McDonnell
CHARLEY FIG	Geoff Morrell
MR TOMASETTI	Christian Manon
DOG PIT CALLER	Douglas Hedge
BELGIAN GIRL	Lucy Knight
BELGIAN BOY	Tobias Saunders
BELGIAN GRANDMOTHER	Marianne Borgo
BELGIAN MOTHER	Vanessa Seydoux
MELODY	Catherine Harvey
PURSER'S ASSISTANT	Ray Macallan
LEVIATHAN STEWARDS	Mark Denny, Andrew Davis
GAMBLING STEWARDS	Paul Rogers, Matt Potter
RABBIT GIRLS	Billie Pluffer, Louella Pluffer
ABORIGINAL BUSKER	David Page
BISHOP DANCER	Norman Kaye
THE DEAN	Michael Duggan
ELDERLY PARISHIONER	Basil Clarke
MRS JUDD	Babs McMillan
MIRIAM CHADWICK	Josephine Byrnes
TREVIS GIRL	Mary Kavanagh
TREVIS BOY	Treffyn Koreshoff

THE VERGER	Patrick Blackwell
MRS MARY HASSET	Lucy Bell
FAN TAN CROUPIER	Wing Hall
FAN TAN PLAYERS	Cassy Huang, Meng Soh
MR JUDD	Chris Haywood
MRS SMITH	Judi Farr
GLASSWORKER	Stuart Campbell
GLASSWORKS FOREMAN	Leslie Dayman
WAITER	Andre Lillis
DINERS	Janet Foye, Dacre King
MR JEFFRIS	Richard Roxburgh
PERCY SMITH	Bille Brown
EXPEDITIONERS	Andrew S. Gilbert, Sandy Winton, Damian Monk
YOUNG CARPENTER	Greg Segal
NARCOO GUIDES	Paul Shillingsworth, Walangari Karntawara
KUMBAINGIRI MEN	Roy Gordon, Kevin Walker, Brett Laurie
MAN IN TAVERN	Steve Rodgers
PUBLICAN'S WIFE	Kim Hillas
ABORIGINAL WOMAN	Elma Kris
MRS TREVIS	Fiona Press
KUMBAINGIRI WOMAN	Elaine Hughes
GOVERNMENT INSPECTOR	Philip Dodd
OSCAR'S SON	Patrick Andrews
OSCAR'S GREAT GRANDSON	Ralph Fiennes
OSCAR'S GREAT-GREAT-GRANDDAUGHTER	Taleah Melenhorst

CREW

First Assistant Director (UK)	Mark Egerton
First Assistant Director	Mark Turnbull
Production Supervisor	Sue Wild
Production Supervisor (UK)	Kathy Sykes
Location Manager	Peter Lawless
Special Effects Supervisor	Steve Courtley
Art Directors	Tom Nursey, John Wingrove
Art Directors (UK)	John Ralph, Paul Ghirardani
Hair & Make-Up Design	Peter Owen
Additional Photography	Russell Boyd A.C.S.
Camera Operator & 2nd Unit	Marc Spicer A.C.S.

Sound Recordist	Ben Osmo
Sound Designer	Andrew Plain
Production Accountant	Jill Steele
Post Production Supervisor	Catherine Knapman

PRODUCED IN ASSOCIATION WITH MERIDIAN FILMS

AUSTRALIAN CREW

Script Supervisor	Victoria Sullivan
Second Assistant Director	Jane Griffin
2nd Second Assistant Director	John Martin
Third Assistant Director	Noni Roy
Unit Manager	Will Matthews
Production Coordinators	Vanessa Brown, Paul Ranford
Assistant Accountant	Sue Collins
Focus Puller	Sally Eccleston
Clapper Loader	Bede Haines
Videosplit Operator	Daniel Pront
Steadicam Operator	Ian McMillan
Underwater Cinematography & 2nd Unit	Rob Hunter
Underwater Camera Assist. & 2nd Unit	Campbell Drummond
Gaffer	Peter Bushby
Best Boy	Iain Mathieson
Electricians	Greg Allen, Ben Steel, Moses Fotofili
Key Grip	Ray Brown
Best Boy Grip	Ian Bird
Grips	Aaron Walker, Steve Wells, Martin Fargher, Sam Newman
Boom Operator	Gerry Nucifora
Sound Assistant/2nd Boom Operator	Nicole Lazaroff
Key Make-Up Artist	Kirsten Veysey
Hair Supervisor	Cheryl Williams
Assistant Make-Up Artist	Bec Taylor
Costume Design Assistant	Michael O'Connor
Costume Supervisor	Jane Johnston
Costume Standby	Heather Laurie
Costume Assistants	Amanda Craze, Carolyn Wells
Costume Cutter	Sheryl Pilkinton

Costume Construction	Judith Meschke, Nick Godlee, Genevieve Blewitt
Set Decorator	Sally Campbell
Set Dressers	Brian Edmonds, Verity Roberts, Sandy Wingrove
Assistant Art Directors	Jacinta Leong, Tony Williams
Art Department Coordinator	Annie Gilhooly
Props Buyer/Dresser	Peter Foster, Arabella Lockhart
Standby Props	Dean Sullivan
Assistant Standby Props	Jan Edwards
Property Master	Brock Sykes
Assistant Property Master	David Crowe
Props Maker	Dick Weight
Assistant Props Makers	Peter Owens, Mark Powell, Tobias Van Leeuwen
Storyboard Artist	Nikki Di Falco
Graphic Artist/Draughtsperson	Helen Baumann
Scenic Artist	Martin Bruveris
Scenic Artist Glass Church	Michael O'Kane
Set Finishers	Matt Connors, Johnny Sella, Ian Merchant, Aiden Guilfoyle
Brush Hand	Joanna Tan
Construction Manager	Greg Hazdu
Construction Foremen	Mark Jones, Jeremy Sparks
Leading Hands	Bruce Fletcher, Eugene Land, Danny Burnett
Head Carpenter	Mark Radcliffe
Carpenters	Steve Toth, Brendan Mullen, Sean Ahern, Ben Turner, Bill Dartnel, Pat Carr, Robert Arthur, Colin Philip
Props Carpenter	Steve Leslie
Steelworker – Foreman	Wayne Porter
Steelworker – Leading Hand	Peter Parry
Steelworkers	Mark Stone, Rodney Nash, Robert Angus, David Korn, Ben Blakebrough, Steve Ross, Robert Campbell, Miles Van Dorssen, Peter Exton, Allan Smith, Chris Axelsen, Rod Young
Trades Assistants	David Rogers, Ron Dean, Scott Magnusson

Construction Assistants	Davor Pavlovic, Ben Foley, Brad Diebert, Orlando Murray
Horse Master	Graham Ware
Wranglers	Kirsten Feddersen, Graham Ware Jnr, Bill Davis
Boat Master	Pat Nash
Armourer	Ken Jones
Greens	Gregg Thomas
Greens Assistants	Angus McDonald, Adrienne Ogle
SFX Technical Coordinator	David Young
SFX Coordinator	Jennifer O'Connell
SFX Technicians	Taj Trengrove, Herman Bron, Rodney Burke, Shane Murphy, Peter Armstrong, Brian Pearce, Brian Belcher, Kim Hilder
SFX Assistants	Kieron O'Connell, Dylan Towner
SFX Dive Master	Bill Collingburn
SFX Divers	Wayne Smith, Geoff Towner, Mick Hinshaw, Graeme Crosskill
Barge Master	Alex Hay
First Assistant Editors	Sam Petty, John Lee
Dialogue Editor	Libby Villa
Dialogue Assistant	Sonal Joshi
Dialogue Editor	Wayne Pashley
Dialogue Assistant	Jenny T. Ward
FX Editor	Jane Paterson
FX Assistant	Nada Mikas
Atmos Editor	Antony Gray
Atmos Assistant	Nick Breslin
Foley Artist	John Simpson
Re-Recording Mixers	Gethin Creagh, Martin Oswin
Music Editor	Bill Bernstein
Music Scoring Mixers	Shawn Murphy, Tom Winslow
Music Mixed By	Tom Winslow
Orchestrator	Thomas Pasatieri
Music Contractor	Leslie Morris
Music Preparation	Julian Bratolyubov
Music Consultant	George Budd
Music Consultant (Aust.)	Christine Woodruff
Music Recorded at	Village Recorder, Paramount Scoring Stage
Music Mixed at	Village Recorder

Extras Casting	Jackie Quilter
Aboriginal Casting	Tracie Walsh
Aboriginal Casting Coordinator	Derek Walker
Stunt Coordinator	Rocky McDonald
Dialogue Coach	Victoria Mielewska
Card Coach	Ron Klinger
Stand-in for Mr Fiennes	Sebastian Hincks
Stand-in for Ms Blanchett	Charmaine Arkley
Production Assistants	Simone O'Halloran, Jonathan Yeo
Accounts Assistant	Stuart McPhee
Producers'/Director's Assistant	Merlyne Jamieson
Director's Assistant	Clancy McDowell
Producers' Assistant	Mel Flanagan
Production Runner	Dimitri Ellerington
Assistant to Mr Fiennes	Becky Veduccio
Art Department Runner	Oleh Sokolovsky
Art Department Assistants	Alice Lodge, Ingrid Weir
Construction Runners	Bill Goodes, Mick Owen
Location Assistant	Anton Denby
Unit Assistants	Peter Kodker, Clem Barrack, Alison Meir, Grayden Le Breton, Erle Dennis, Neil Faulkner, Jim Davidson
Unit Nurse	Patsy Buchan
Catering	Johnny Faithful
Unit Publicity	Rea Francis Media
Unit Photographer	Philip Le Mesurier

UK PRODUCTION SERVICES SUPPLIED BY ARTISAN FILMS

UK CREW

Location Managers	Angus More-Gordon, Andrew Hill
Unit Manager	Reggie Blain
Production Coordinator	Dervn Stafford
Producers' Assistant	Alison Odell
Production Accountant	Rachel James
Assistant Accountant	Sarah Kaye
Second Assistant Director	Clare Awdry
Crowd Casting	Victoria Connell
Third Assistant Director	Caspar Campbell
Camera Grip	Gary Romaine
Steadicam & 2nd Unit Photography	Nigel Kirton

Steadicam Operator	John Ward
Clapper Loader/2nd Focus Puller	Nick Watt
Clapper Loader	Rachel MacGregor
Gaffer	Terry Edland
Best Boy	Ashley Palin
Electricians	Paul Kemp, Mark Evans, Chris Bailey
Generator Operator	Danny Young
Costume Design Assistant	Debbie Scott
Wardrobe Supervisor	Marion Weise
Wardrobe Mistress	Jane Petrie
Wardrobe Master	Nigel Egerton
Wardrobe Assistant	June Nevin
Make-Up/Hair Assistants	Nikita Rae, Paul Gooch
Property Buyer	Trisha Edwards
Assistant Set Dresser	Philippa Hart
Assistant Property Buyer	Katherine Hooker
Prop Master	Arthur Wicks
Draughtsperson	Gary Tomkins
Chargehand Standby	Mark Fruin
Chargehand Dressing Propman	Mark McNiel
Dressing Props	Antonio Muner
Standby Propman	Sean McConvill
Prop Storeman	Stan Cook
Boat Master	Tony Tucker – Anchor Marine
SFX Coordinator	Joss Williams
Wire Man	Bob Wiesinger
Stunt Coordinator	Graeme Crowther
Construction Manager	John Hedges
Supervising Carpenter	Roger Willis
Supervising Painter	Michael Guyett
Standby Carpenter	Richard Jones
Standby Painter	Jim Ede
Standby Stagehand	Alan Titmus
Standby Rigger	Alan Perez
Second Boom Operator	Bradley Kendrick
Assistant Editor	Rob Ireland
Assistant Production Coordinator	Joan Thompson
Production Runner	Karina Lawson
Floor Runner	Joel Hopkins
Art Department Runners	Candida Lloyd, Alexandra Walker
Unit Nurse	Caroline Quilter

Gambling Consultant	Marten Julian
Unit Publicity	Corbett & Keene
Unit Photographer	Stephen F. Morley
Laboratory & Mixing Facility	Atlab Australia
Lab Liaison	Ian Russell
Pos Conforms	Karen Psaltis
Neg Cutting	Kerry Ferguson, Margaret Bourke
Grading	Arthur Cambridge
Digital Imaging & Optical Effects	Dfilm Services
Digital Effects Manager	Robert Sandeman
Optical Effects Manager	Roger Cowland
Creative Director	Peter Doyle
Digital Artist	Elizabeth Carlon
Effects Make-Up/Printing	Ken Phelan
Scanning & Recording Supervisor	Anthos Simon
Scanning Operator	John Pope
Title Design	Belinda Bennetts
Titles & Shooting	Optical & Graphic
Camera Equipment	Samuelson Film Service, Bill Ross
Editing & ADR Facility	Spectrum Films
ADR/Foley Recordist	Rick Lisle
Telecine Transfers	Digital Pictures, Claudio Sepulveda
ADR Facility (UK)	De Lane Lea Sound Centre
ADR Mixer & Recordist	Ted Swanscott, Terry Isted
Voice Casting (UK)	Brendan Donnison for Lyps Inc.
Legal Representation (Aust.)	Tress Cocks & Maddox
(UK)	Campbell Hooper
Completion Guarantor	Film Finances, Inc.
Liaison	Adrienne Read
Production Consultant	Helen Watts
Accounting (Aust.)	Moneypenny Services
Insurance	Aon Entertainment Risk Services
Travel & Accommodation	Showtravel Internet Travel

NO ANIMALS WERE INJURED IN THE MAKING OF THIS FILM

THE PRODUCERS WISH TO THANK

Arthur Sanderson & Sons – Osborne & Little – Qantas – People of the Clarence River Valley & State Emergency Services – The National Trust – Art Gallery of New South Wales – National Parks & Wildlife Service of New South Wales

Motet – Os Justi
Written by Anton Bruckner
Performed by La Chapelle Royale
/Collegium Vocale/Ensemble
Musique Oblique
Dir. Philippe Herreweghe
Courtesy Harmonia Mundi S.A.,
France

Haec Dies
Written by John Sheppard
Performed by The Choir of
King's College, Cambridge
Conducted by Philip Ledger
Courtesy EMI Records UK
and EMI Music Australia Pty. Ltd.

Motetten Lobet de Herrn,
Alle Heiden BMV 230
Written by Johann Sebastian Bach
Performed by Rostocker
Motettenchor/Capella Fidicinia
Leipzig
Hartwig Eschenburg
Courtesy Capriccio Digital

Fantasia in C Minor for Piano,
Chorus & Orchestra, Op. 80
Written by Ludwig Van Beethoven
Performed by Jan Panenka – Piano
Prague Radio Chorus/Milan Maly
Prague Symphony Orchestra
Conducted by Vaclav Smetacek

Soundtrack album available on Sony Classical

This film was developed with the assistance of New South Wales Film
and Television Office, NSW Film and TV Office Sydney, Australia

Script developed with the assistance of the Australian Film Commission

Released by
Twentieth Century Fox